CONSCIOUS CRAFTS

KNITTING

Leaping Hare Press

First published in 2022 by Leaping Hare Press,
an imprint of The Quarto Group.
The Old Brewery, 6 Blundell Street
London, N7 9BH,
United Kingdom
T (0)20 7700 6700
www.QuartoKnows.com

A catalogue record for this book is available from the British Library.

ISBN 978-0-7112-6604-9
Ebook ISBN 978-0-7112-6605-6

10 9 8 7 6 5 4 3 2 1

Commissioning Editor Monica Perdoni
Designer Ginny Zeal
Illustrators Cathy Brear and Stuart Edwards
Model Vanessa Asare
Photographer Kingsley Koranteng

Printed in China

MIX
Paper from responsible sources
FSC® C016973
FSC www.fsc.org

Conscious Crafts

KNITTING

20 MINDFUL MAKES TO RECONNECT HEAD, HEART & HANDS

Sicgmone Kludje and Vanessa Koranteng

Leaping Hare Press

contents

introduction

As creative collaborators we've always had the passion to plan, develop and execute projects and we've always worked well together. Our ideas embrace stories and the meanings behind each project. Each of these 20 makes will touch on various zones of your wellbeing, most importantly your space, additions to your look and knitting techniques that you can learn that can then be applied to other projects.

Knitting has been proven to relax us; the repetitive actions help us to think clearly and positively and can even lead to curing pain in relation to physical and constant mental battles, "It's here to help us find a joyous sense of awareness, where repetitive stress no longer affects us," (Matthews, 2016). The strength of the mind is underestimated because even when we do make things we realize that our thoughts wonder and it's so easy to let our minds run rather than use it. The aim of this book is to create a productive environment for yourself, slowly repeat the steps resulting in a creation you've made with love.

Creativity has been a large part of our lives ever since we have been in school, with Sicgmone studying art at GCSE and A-level to graduating in textile design at Central Saint Martins, which led to designing a knitwear fashion label called Sicgmoné and currently becoming a lecturer in Textile Design at University of Arts London. The impact of conveying an in-depth textile knowledge to students has always been an important part of her role in empowering and teaching the future generation of designers.

Vanessa has always been intrigued by art and textiles, exploring summer schools doing screen print workshops to fashion design and ceramics in school to graduating from University of Brighton studying Architectural Technology where she has currently amassed over 8+ years in the built environment and Interior design industry, being able to complete million-pound projects for clients. Alongside that she continued to allow her creativity to flourish by also developing a second hand/ vintage garment label called Brantuo Studio where she would scour warehouses, collect, style and shoot these and turn this around into collections month on month.

These experiences collectively have helped us to enjoy the art of craft and the importance of being able to create unique items using our hands. The connection to the process of creating textiles opens up the space of meditation, it settles the mind while being excited to cherish a new connection to our heritage.

This lead to us founding, Black Girl Knit Club. Established in 2019, our mission as friends turned business partners is to empower and encourage Black women in craft, to create something with their hands and embrace their identity. We don't venture far away from what we have gotten to love, which is crafts and hand skills. We both had the urge to find a safe and inclusive space for us to develop skills with every workshop we teach; for everyone to go away with something, to embrace their personal touch to each project. It was vital to our wellbeing to be in the space with likeminded people who look like us, who are of similar cultures and embracing their identity, too. We also wanted to create a sacred space that produces a happy knitter. The space is built around the heart of creativity and not isolation, escapism and the relief knitting provides from mundane everyday life and justifies the fruitful time spent away from it.

We wanted to highlight the importance of wellbeing and mindfulness when knitting together by noting the emotions it brings when you make something for the first time. As time goes on we get busier everyday and we rarely carve out the time to concentrate on ourselves and achieving that is the luxury we want to bring to you. When we knit we always glance at the stitches and pattern very intricately, we have to concentrate on what we're doing but relax at the same time. We can do this by watching our hands create tension, controlling our breathing and monitoring our thoughts. In fact, we capture our thoughts peacefully and go to the otherside to a deeper, more insightful place of creativity.

In this book we really want to enhance and bring out various types of experiences as you create these 20 makes for different areas of your life that will spark joy and value your inner calm. These projects were designed for all ages and levels in mind and our hope is for you to enjoy this time of slow crafts and the possibility to feel more relaxed by the time you put your needles down.

References:
Conscious Crafts – Pottery by Lucy Davidson (2021). *The Mindfulness in Knitting* by Rachel Matthews (2016)

tools and equipment

There are several essential tools that you will need before you can explore the exciting knit designs in this book. These are the basic tools and equipment you will need for most knitted projects.

Knitting needles Straight knitting needles are the basic tool used to create any hand-knitted piece. They can be purchased in a variety of sizes and are usually made from plastic, steel or wood – deciding which type to use is down to personal preference. Yarn ball bands always include a recommended needle size for the yarn and most knitting patterns will include a suggested yarn weight and needle size, so make sure you check these before you start your knitting projects.

Circular knitting needles Circular knitting needles have two tips made from metal, plastic or wood that are joined together by a length of flexible plastic cording. They are available in a range of lengths and are ideal for knitting sweaters, socks, mittens and other accessories that are worked in a continuous round.

Crochet hooks A crochet hook can be used for weaving different yarn threads into your knitted projects; for example, a crochet hook is used to add fringing for the Fringed Scarf (see page 112).

Tape measure You will need this essential piece of kit to check the tension (gauge) on your knitted pieces (see page 43). A tape measure is also helpful for checking the sizing of any knitted work in progress.

Pins You will need pins when seaming to hold the edges in place. They are also helpful for marking out an area when checking your tension (gauge). Try to find pins with large heads, so that they are visible between the knitted stitches and don't slip through and get lost too easily.

Stitch holders Stitch holders are used to hold open stitches while they are not being worked on the knitting needles. For example, they can be used when shaping the neckline of a sweater. Stitch holders are available in different colours and sizes.

Stitch markers Stitch markers are little round gadgets made from either metal or plastic. They have multiple uses: they are used to mark the end of a row when knitting in the round; they can be placed onto a knitting needle to highlight a certain place in a row; or used to temporarily hold a dropped stitch while you are knitting.

Row counter Row counters can be used to keep track of your completed stitches and rows. They slip easily onto the knitting needle, and you just need to remember to turn the dial after each row.

Tapestry needle A tapestry needle is a blunt-tipped sewing needle that can go easily through any knit stitch. The large eye allows for different weights of yarn to be threaded through it. This is the needle most commonly used for seaming and for weaving in any loose ends.

Needle gauge Most knitting needles have their size printed on them; however, others may not be correctly marked or not marked at all. A needle gauge is very useful for double checking you have the correct needle size.

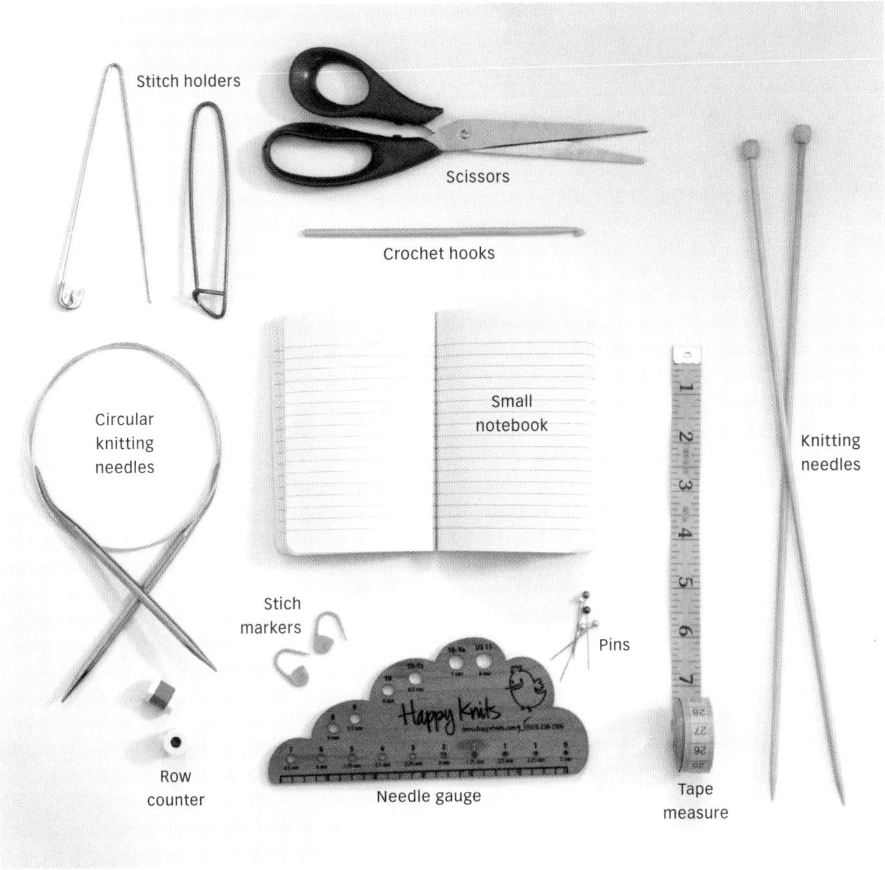

Pom-pom maker Pom-pom makers are designed for creating yarn pom-poms. They are available in a range of different sizes and can be used with yarn of any thickness. The most commonly available sizes are: 3.5cm (1½in), 5.5cm (2¼in), 7cm (2¾in) and 9cm (3½in) diameters.

Scissors You will need a pair of scissors to cut the yarn during the projects. Small or medium size scissors are most useful as they can be used for delicate snipping.

Small notebook A small notebook is useful for recording any small changes you may have made to a pattern while knitting. They are also useful for taking notes on best practice for working with particular yarns or techniques for the first time.

knitting basics

making a slipknot

Every piece of knitting begins with a slipknot. The slipknot counts as the first stitch on your needle.

1 Loop your yarn as if to make a knot, leaving a tail of your desired length – about 10cm (4in) in length.

2 Use the knitting needle tip to catch the yarn inside the loop.

3 Continue by tightening the knot on the needle. This is your first stitch.

1

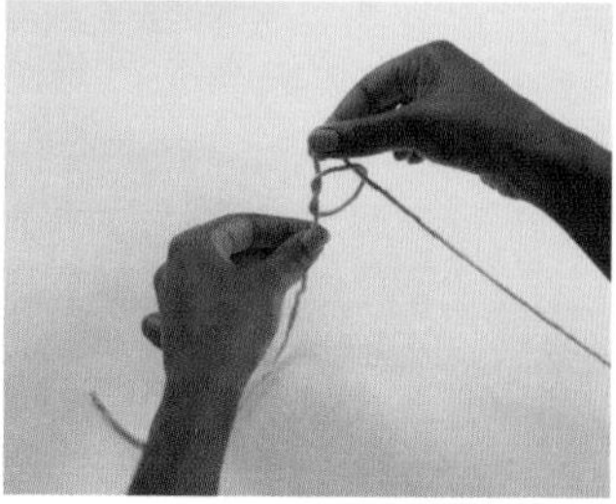

2

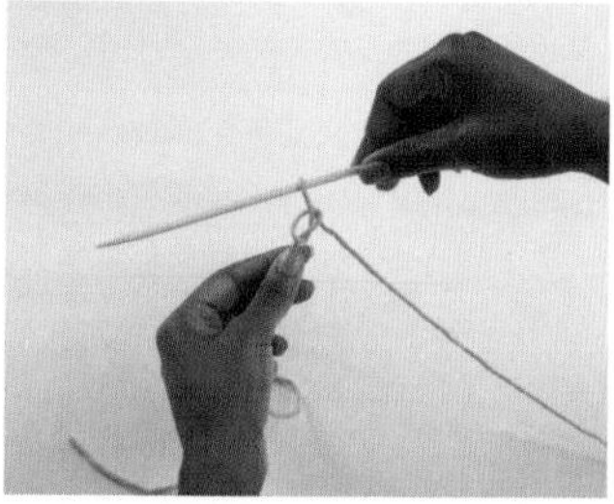

3

knitted cast on

The knitted cast on creates a very neat edge to your knitting, and is suitable for most projects. Every stitch is pulled through the previous loop. This gives the cast on edge extra strength.

1

2

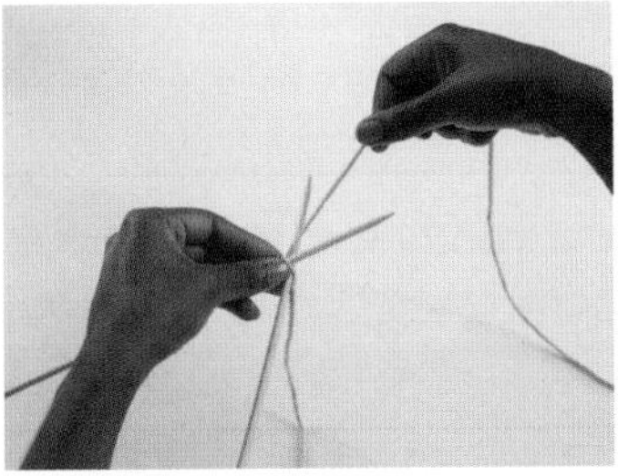

3

4

1 Make a slipknot as shown opposite and hold the needle with the slipknot in your left hand. To knit the first stitch, insert the right-hand (RH) needle through the first stitch (slipknot) from left through to right.

2 Wrap the yarn around the RH tip from right to left (anticlockwise). Pull the new loop through the stitch on the left-hand (LH) needle.

3 Place the stitch back on the LH needle. You now have two stitches.

4 Continue to cast on by inserting the RH needle into the next stitch on the LH needle, wrapping the yarn around the tip of the RH needle and pulling the loop of the wrapped yarn through the stitch with the tip of the RH needle. Then place the stitch on the LH needle. Repeat until you have the required number of stitches.

long-tail cast on

This easy cast on knitting technique creates a stretchy elastic edge, which is necessary for some projects. The long-tail cast on is often used to start the hems and cuffs on a sweater.

1

2

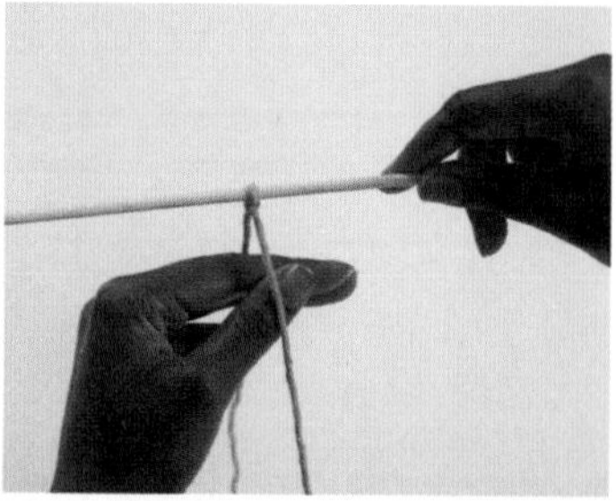

3

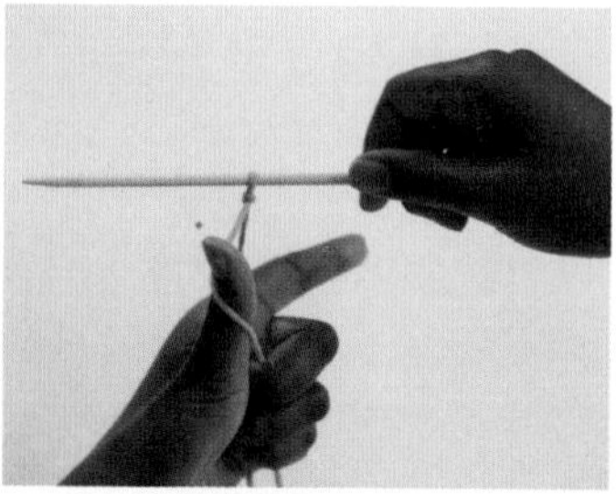

4

1 Create a slipknot leaving a very long yarn tail (see page 12). Place the slipknot on the RH needle.

2 Insert your index finger and thumb between the two strands of yarn.

3 Wrap your remaining three fingers around the two hanging yarn strands and grip firmly. Spread your index finger and thumb and hold open, keeping a slight tension on the yarn strands.

4 Insert your needle under the yarn strand near your thumb and lift the strand with the needle. Pull the strand up and do not remove it.

6

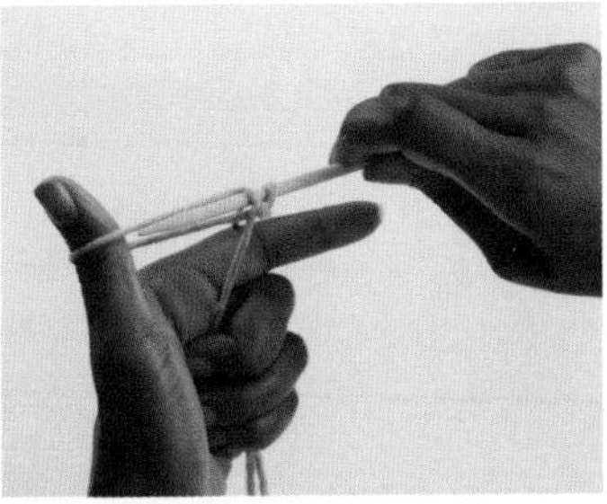

7

8

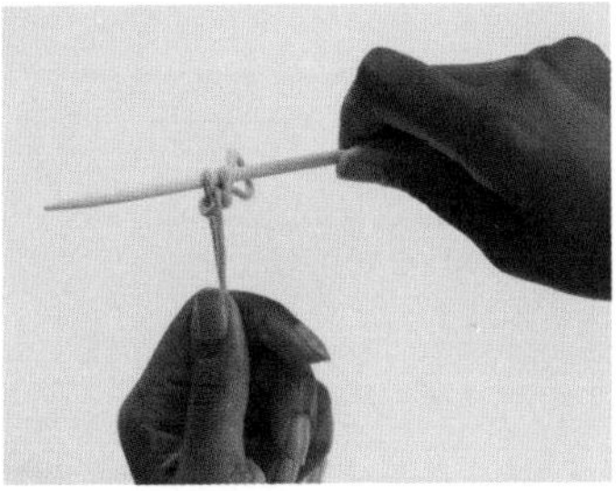

5 With the lifted strand still on the needle, take the needle over the upper strand, which is tensioned on the index finger, and bring this loop through the loop on the thumb.

6 Pull the strand through the loop opening near the thumb.

7 Remove your thumb from the strand and pull down on both yarn strands until the stitch is firmly positioned on the needle. Repeat steps 1 to 7 for each stitch you need to cast on.

knit stitch (k)

The knit stitch is one of the basic fundamental stitches used in most knitting patterns. Once you have mastered this stitch, you can work and follow different stitch patterns. Practice the knit stitch until you produce a good square swatch.

1

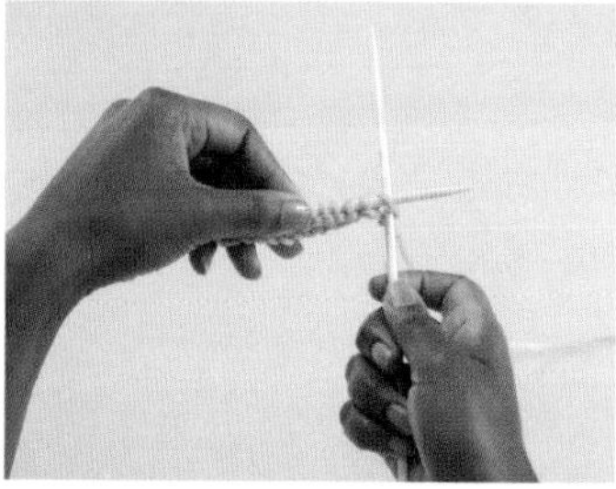

2

3

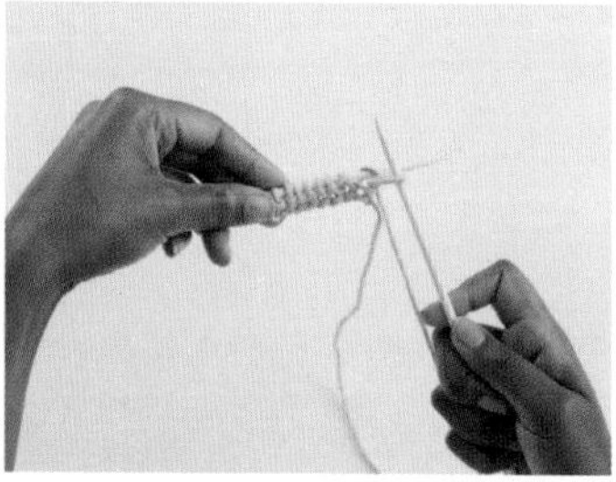

4

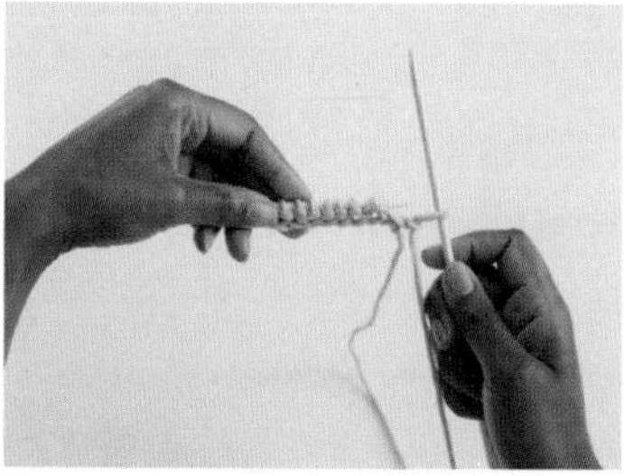

1 Hold the needle with the cast-on stitches in your left hand.

2 Insert the RH needle from left to right through the front of the first stitch on your LH needle.

3 Wrap the yarn from left to right over the end of the RH needle. Pull the yarn through the stitch, this will form a new stitch on the RH needle.

4 Drop the original stitch off the LH needle and keep the new stitch on the RH needle. Repeat steps 1 to 3 until all stitches on the LH needle have been worked.

continental knit stitch

The continental knit method differs slightly from the traditional knit method. You hold both the yarn and the stitches in your left hand. This method is favoured in mainland Europe.

1

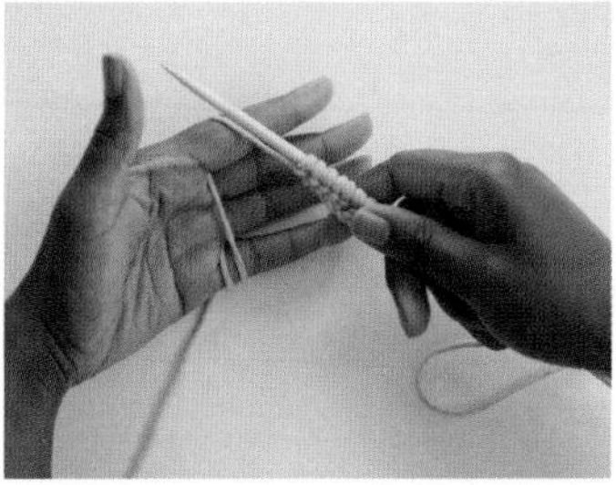

2

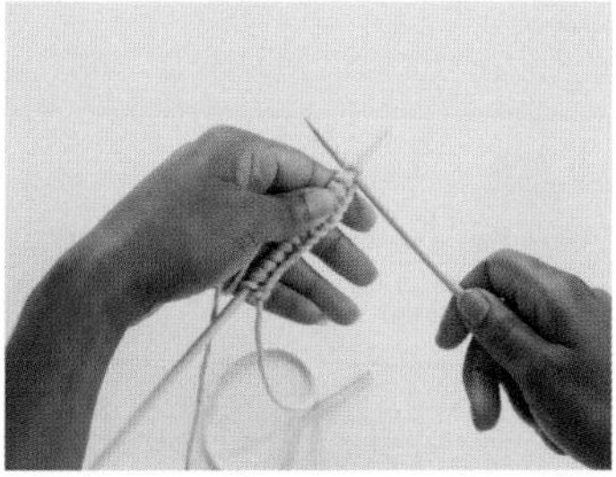

3

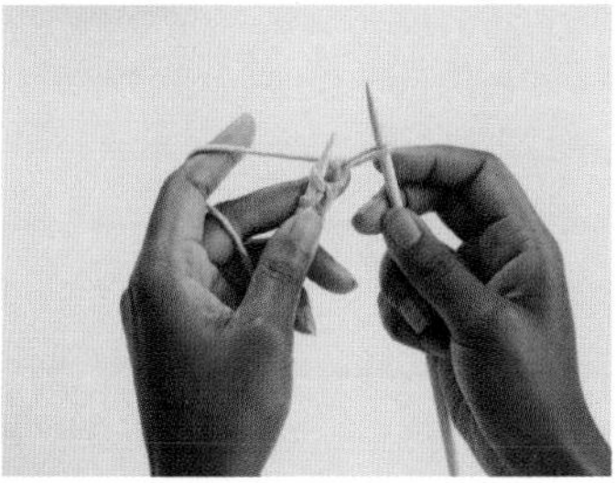

4

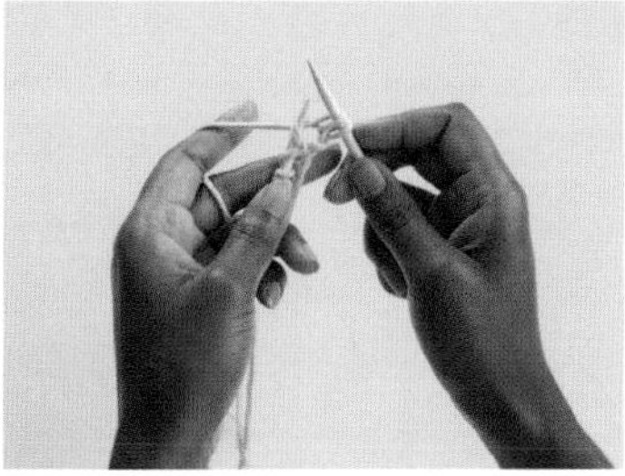

1 Hold the needle with the stitches in your right hand. Wrap the yarn around your left pinkie and index finger. Move the needle to your left hand.

2 Insert the RH needle from left to right through the front of the first stitch on the LH needle. Lay the yarn across the RH needle tip from left to right using your left index finger.

3 Use the RH needle tip to pull the yarn through the stitch, this will then form a new stitch on the RH needle.

4 Drop the original stitch off the LH needle and keep the new stitch on the RH needle. Repeat steps 2–4 until all stitches on the LH needle have been worked.

purl stitch (p)

The purl stitch is the second basic stitch that you will learn. The knit and purl stitch are the basic stitches used in all knitting patterns. For the purling technique, the yarn is held at the front of the work in front of the needles.

1

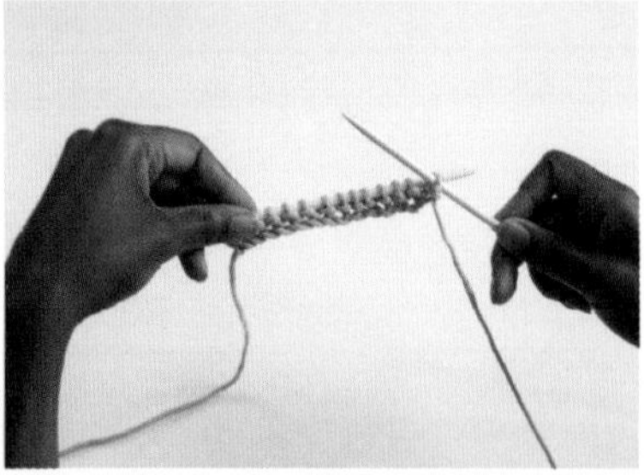

2

3

4

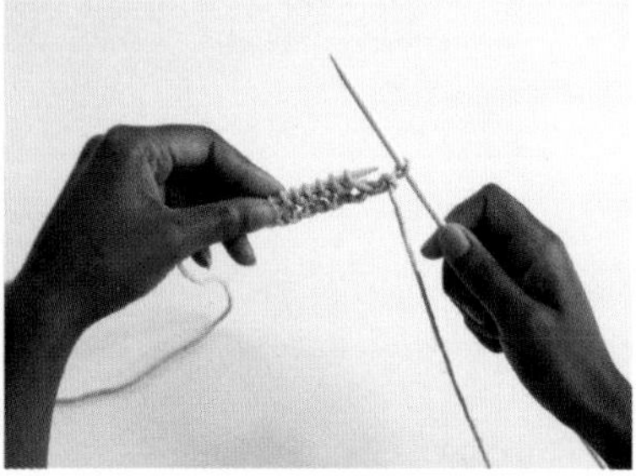

1 Hold the needle with the cast-on stitches in your left hand and with the working yarn at the front. Insert the RH needle from right to left into the front of the first stitch on the LH needle.

2 Wrap the yarn from right to left (anticlockwise) over the RH needle.

3 Pull the yarn through the stitch, forming a new stitch on the RH needle.

4 Drop the original stitch off the LH needle and keep the new stitch on the RH needle. Repeat steps 1 to 4 until all stitches on the LH needle have been worked.

continental purl stitch

You can also purl using the continental method.

1

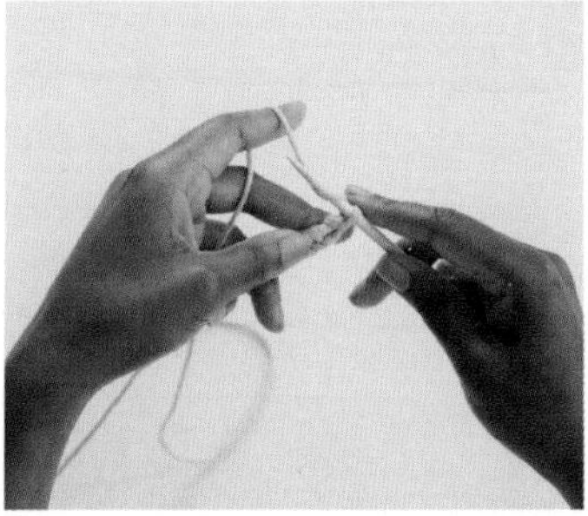

2

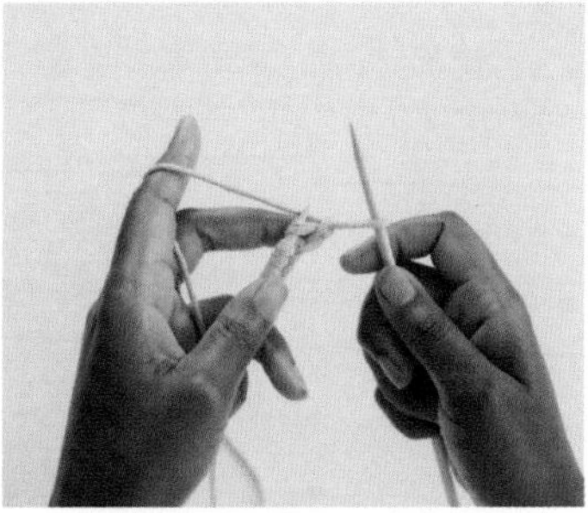

1 Hold the yarn and the needle with the cast-on stitches in your left hand. With the working yarn at the front, insert the RH needle from right to left through the front of the first stitch on the LH needle. Wrap the yarn from right to left (anticlockwise) over the RH needle using your left index finger.

2 Use the RH needle tip to pull the yarn through the stitch, this will then form a new stitch on the RH needle. Drop the original stitch off the LH needle and keep the new stitch on the RH needle. Repeat steps 1–2 until all stitches on the LH needle have been worked.

garter stitch

This simple stitch pattern is produced by knitting every row.

1 Cast on the required number of stitches. (see pages 13–15).

2 Knit to end (see Knit Stitch, page 16).

3 Repeat this row to form the pattern and until you reach the desired length.

stocking (stockinette) stitch

Stocking stitch is produced by knitting all the stitches on the right-side rows and purling on the wrong-side rows.

1 Cast on the required number of stitches (see pages 13–15).

2 Row 1: (RS) Knit to end (see page 16).

3 Row 2: Purl to end (see page 18).

Repeat steps 1 and 2 to the required length.

moss stitch (seed stitch)

Moss stitch is a two-row pattern repeat. You knit one (see page 16), purl one (see page 18), alternated across the row. The order of the pattern also changes depending on whether you have an even or odd number of stitches on your knitting needles.

1

2

3

4

Even number of stitches

1 Cast on an even number of stitches.

2 Row 1: (RS) *K1, p1, repeat from * to the end.

3 Row 2: * P1, k1, repeat from * to the end.

Repeat rows 1 and 2 to form the pattern and until you reach the desired length.

Odd number of stitches

1 Cast on an odd number of stitches.

2 Row 1: K1, *p1, k1 – repeat from * to the end.

3 Repeat this row to form the pattern and until you reach the desired length.

basketweave stitch

Basketweave stitch is created using a combination of knit and purl stitches, which creates a woven basket-like texture effect.

1

2

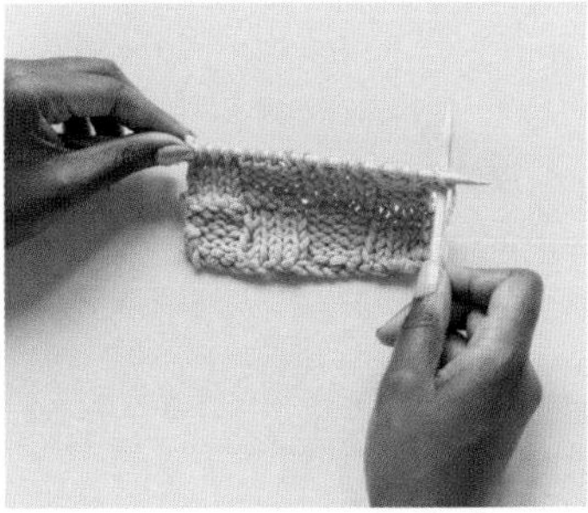

3

4

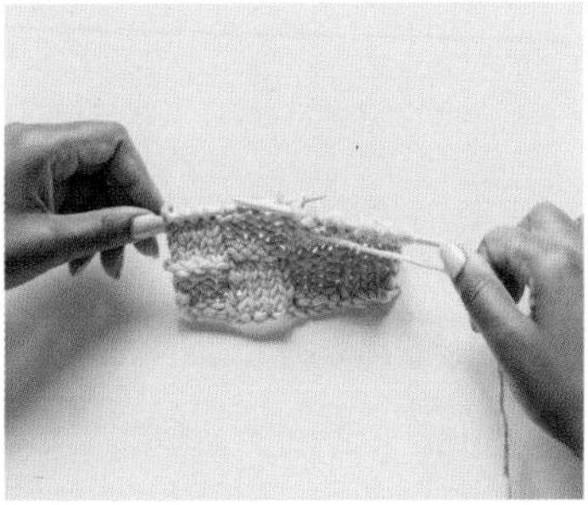

1 Cast on a multiple of 8 stitches. In this case, a total of 16 stitches.

2 Begin the basketweave stitch pattern:
Row 1: (RS) k4, p4, rep from * to end.
Row 2: as row 1.
Row 3: as row 1.
Row 4: as row 1.

3 Row 5: *p4, k4, rep from * to end.
Row 6: as row 5.
Row 7: as row 5.
Row 8: as row 5.

4 Repeat steps 2–3 until you reach the desired length.

garter ridge stitch

The garter ridge stitch is made of alternative rows of knit and purl stitches with a garter stitch ridge every three rows. This forms an interesting texture of a horizontal line of raised bumps across the knit.
raised bumps across the knit.

1

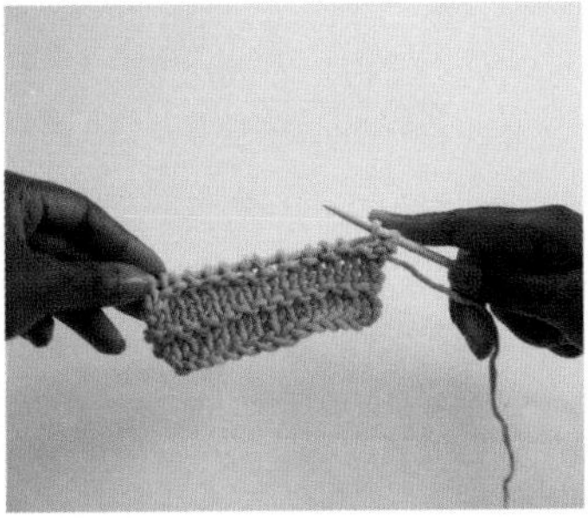

2

3

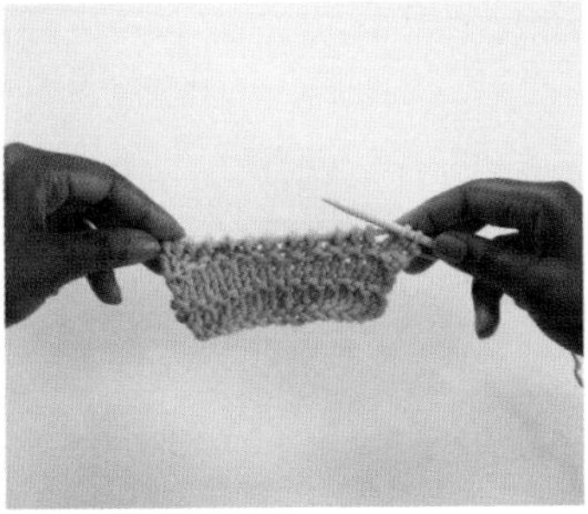

4

1 Cast on 14 stitches.

2 Row 1: (RS) Knit to the end of the row.
Row 2: Purl to the end of the row.
Row 3: Knit to the end of the row.
Row 4: Knit to the end of the row.

3 Repeat rows 1–4 until you reach the desired length.

large garter ridge stitch

The large garter ridge stitch is created by alternate knit and purl rows with three garter stitch ridges made by repeating purl rows. This stitch is a very neat alternative to plain garter stitch and can be used for scarves, garments or blankets.

1

2

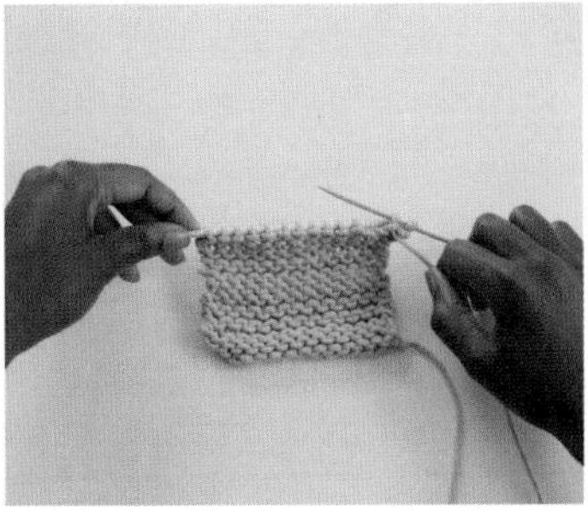

3

4

1 Cast on 13 stitches.

2 Row 1: (RS) Knit to the end of the row.
Row 2: Purl to the end of the row.
Row 3: Knit to the end of the row.
Rows 5–10: Purl to the end of the row.

3 Repeat rows 1–10 rows to form the pattern until you reach the desired length.

1 x 1 rib stitch

The 1 x 1 rib stitch is mostly used at the beginning or at the end of a piece of knitting, to prevent any edges from curling over. It is often used for sweater hems, cuffs and necklines.

Even number of stitches

Cast on an even number of stitches; for example, 16 stitches .
Row 1: *K1, p1, rep from * to end.
Repeat this row to form the pattern and until you reach the desired length.

Odd number of stitches

Cast on an odd number of stitches.
Row 1: K1, *p1, k1, rep from * to end.
Row 2: P1, *k1, p1, rep from * to end.
Repeat rows 1 and 2 to form the pattern and until you reach the desired length.

1

2

2 x 2 rib stitch

The 2x2 rib stitch forms a more elastic and chunkier rib than 1x1 rib stitch. It can be worked as a 1 row or a 2 row repeat; both versions have an even number of stitches. This stitch also prevents edges from rolling over.

1 row repeat

Cast on a multiple of 4 stitches; for example, 16 stitches.
Row 1: *K2, p2, rep from * to the end of the row.
Repeat this row to form the pattern and until you reach the desired length.

2 row repeat

Cast on a multiple of 4 plus 2; for example, 14 stitches.
Row 1: K2, *p2, k2, rep from * to the end of the row.
Row 2: P2, *k2, p2, rep from * to the end of the row.
Repeat rows 1 and 2 to form the pattern and until you reach the desired length.

1

2

changing colour

When you come to the end of the ball of yarn or when a pattern asks you to change the yarn colour, the next step is to join in a new ball of yarn so that you can continue knitting.

1 Tie the new yarn into a loose knot around the yarn that you have on the needles.

2 Slide the new yarn knot up until it touches the knitting needle.

3 Pull the tail ends of the new yarn to secure the knot.

4 Now simply start knitting with the new yarn.

5 When you have changed yarn your work will have some loose yarn ends (little tails). These need to be woven into your knitting to secure them and prevent your knitting from unravelling (see page 40).

1

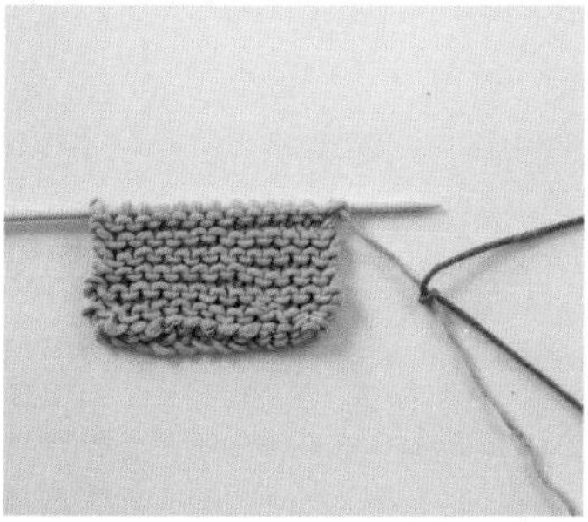

2

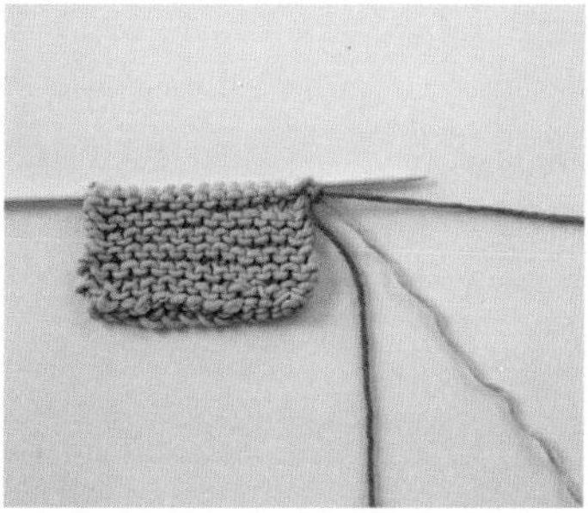

3

4

5

casting (binding) off

Casting off is the term used for finishing off your knitting so that you have a neat edge that will not unravel.

1

2

3

4

1 Knit two stitches.

2 Insert the tip of the LH needle into the first stitch knitted on the RH needle.

3 Take the first stitch over the second stitch and drop this off your RH needle. You will then have one stitch on the RH needle.

4 Knit one more stitch so that you have two stitches on your RH knitting needle and repeat steps 2–4 until one last stitch remains. Remember that you should only have one or two stitches on the RH needle at any time. To finish casting off, cut your yarn leaving a 10cm (4in) tail and take the tail of the yarn through the loop to fasten off. You have now cast off all of your stitches.

joining techniques

mattress stitch on stocking (stockinette) stitch

Mattress stitch can be used to join two pieces of knitting together. This creates an invisible seam and is mostly used for sewing vertical seams, such as those on sweaters. Mattress stitch can be used for seaming stocking stitch (see page 21) and garter stitch (see page 20).

If you look at a sample of stocking stitch, you will see that each knit stitch creates a V shape. Between every V shape there are horizontal bars running between the stitches. You will sew under these bars when working mattress stitch.

1

2

3

4

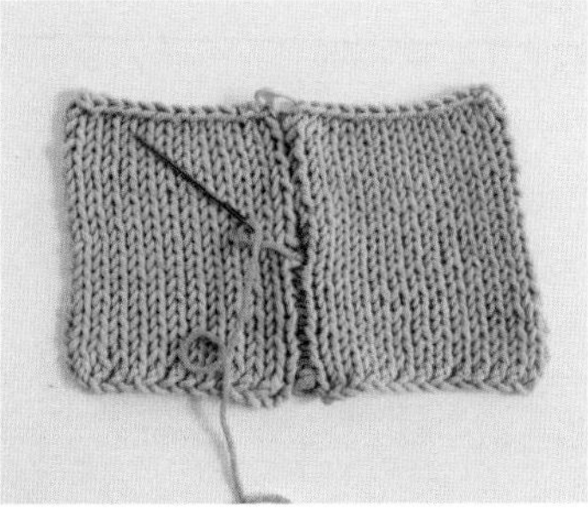

1 Lay your two pieces of knitting down with the right side facing you.

2 Thread your tapestry needle and join your yarn to the LH piece just above the cast-on edge. Take your needle over to the RH piece and insert your needle from the front under the first horizontal bar just above the cast-on edge, bringing it out to the front again.

3 Now sew under the corresponding horizontal bar on the LH piece.

4 Repeat steps 2 and 3. Continue working the yarn vertically along the two edges, taking the tapestry needle under each horizontal bar.

5 You can pull both ends of the yarn to completely close the seam.

flat seam stitch

This seam can be used to join two knitted pieces together and differs slightly from mattress stitch. In this book, this style of seam is mainly for joining moss stitch pieces (see page 22).

1

2

3

4

1 Place the pieces to be joined together edge-to- edge, wrong side facing upwards and the cast-on or cast-off edges together. Thread your tapestry needle and join your yarn to the LH piece just below edge.

2 Take your needle from left to right through the first edge loop on the LH piece. Insert your needle from left to right through the corresponding edge loop on the RH piece. Pull the yarn through.

3 Now insert your needle from right to left through the RH edge loop directly above the one just used and from right to left through the corresponding edge loop on the LH piece. Pull the yarn through.

4 Insert the needle from left to right through the LH edge loop directly above the one just used and from left to right through the corresponding edge loop on the RH piece. Pull the yarn through. Repeat steps 3 and 4. Continue working the yarn along the two edges, taking the tapestry needle under each edge loop.

weaving in ends

After you cast off a piece of knitting, you will almost always have one or more yarn tails to weave into your knitting. To get rid of your loose ends without ruining your work, you cannot just cut them off with scissors, you will need to sew or 'weave' them into your project.

1

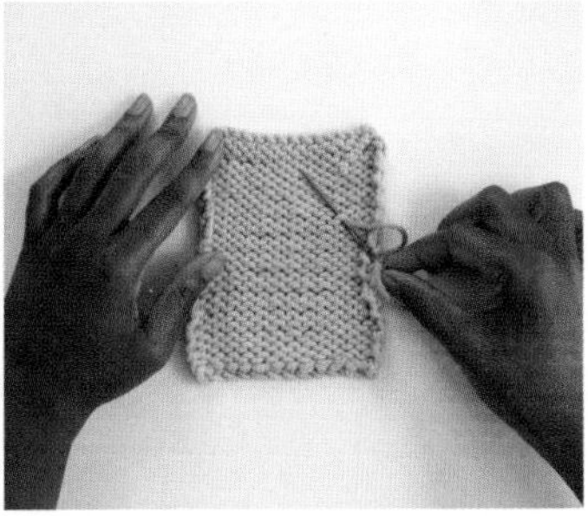

2

3

4

1 Thread the loose end through the eye of a tapestry needle.

2 At the back of your knitting, garter stitch creates ridges of purl bumps. One slightly above the other with the bottom bump creating a smiley face. Insert your needle under the top purl bump.

3 Pull the needle and tail end through the top bump.

4 Rotate your needle and push it under the adjacent purl bump, it is slightly lower and makes more of a smiley face.

5 Again, rotate the needle upwards and through the adjacent purl bump.

6 Continue with steps 3 and 4 for several more stitches, until the tail end is secure.

finishing techniques

Blocking

Blocking is the final step of finishing your project. Once you have blocked your knitting this should even out your stitches and give your project a professional finished look. You can test your blocking on your tension swatch piece before doing this on your final knitted item.

Wet blocking

When blocking your swatch or final work, you should use a very light shampoo – fill up the sink with warm water and allow the swatch to soak for at least 15–20 minutes. When you remove the swatch, squeeze out any excess water. You can also use a towel to do this.

Lay the swatch on a flat surface (you can also use pins to help with this). Allow the piece to dry completely.

Steam blocking

Steam blocking is a way to shape your knitted pieces. When you steam block a piece of knitting, you steam it into its final shape instead of using water (see opposite).

1 Pin the item to a flat surface; you can slightly spread your knitted piece to the correct measurements if needed. (See knitted sample, step 4 on page 111.)

2 Use a steam iron over the knitted swatch/piece about an 2.5cm (1in) away from the surface. Move the iron steam up and down along fabric so the steam penetrates through the knit. Make sure the iron doesn't touch the knit as this may ruin the fabric.

Also avoid steam blocking acrylic yarns or fancy yarns. Always check the care labels as these may felt or melt slightly from the iron heat.

abbreviations

Here are a list of abbreviations used throughout this book. These are also some of the most commonly used knitting abbreviations, which will help you to follow knitting patterns. They can appear as upper or lower case letters but will mean the same however they are written:

K	Knit	**Sts**	Stitches	**YB**	Yarn back
P	Purl	**Rep**	Repeat	**LH**	Left hand
Kw	Knitwise	**Tog**	Together	**RH**	Right hand
Pw	Purlwise	**K2tog**	Knit two stitches together	**RS**	Right side
St	Stitch	**YF**	Yarn forward	**WS**	Wrong side

knitting tension (gauge)

Tension refers to the number of stiches and rows per centimetre (inch) of a particular project pattern. Every knitting pattern that you use will outline the tension that you should knit with and the recommended knitting needle size.

In order to make sure that your tension is the same as in the pattern, you should create a small knitted swatch. A swatch is a little test sample using the yarn and needles recommended in the knit pattern. This will ensure that your finished piece will be the correct size and tension – so not too tight or too loose.

1 Check the tension listed in the initial pattern and make sure you use the recommended knitting needle size and yarn. It is suggested that you cast on at least 10 stitches more than needed when checking your tension square.For example, if the pattern says that 7sts and 13 rows = 10cm (4in) stocking stitch. You should cast on at least 17sts and knit for more than 13 rows, this will ensure that your tension measurement is more accurate as it will be easier to measure.

2 When you have finished knitting your tension square, block it (see page 111, step 4) and allow the knit to try. This will give a more accurate tension measurement.

3 Use a measuring tape or a special tension tool to count the number of stitches and rows that are in 10cm (4in) across the knitted swatch. To be more precise use two pins to mark 10cm (4in) on the swatch and count each stitch between the pins. Also remember if you are counting stitches in garter, each smiley curve is a stitch. In stocking stitch on the 'right side' of the fabric every V on the fabric is also a stitch.

4 If you knit your tension swatch and the number of stitches and rows match the pattern, then you can continue knitting the project. However, if the tension measurements do not match then you will need to knit the swatch again until they are exact.

If you have more stitches than suggested this indicates that the tension is tight and you should try larger knitting needles. Begin with going one needle size up, so if the pattern stated 6mm (US10) needles try creating another swatch with 7mm needles.

Alternatively, if you have fewer stitches than required, your tension is probably too loose and you should go down a needle size. You will often have to try creating a few different swatches before getting the correct tension.

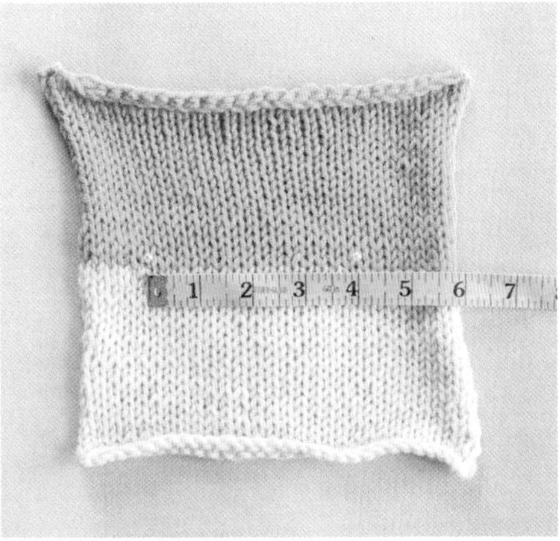

I am grateful for the
home I have, knowing
that at this moment,
all I have is all I need

At home you can truly be yourself because you are surrounded by the spaces you've personally curated to shelter in, rest in, enjoy and love. Lived experiences are attached to each space and each room, including beautiful memories, which contribute to the experience of living in your own home.

The makes in this section are designed to touch each section of your home and to allow you to create a connecting style between all the different spaces: living room, office, kitchen, dining room and bedroom. Intertwining the style of the different spaces in your home using crafts and creativity can be truly beneficial to wellbeing and we hope each of these enjoyable projects will contribute to your overall wellness.

teacup coasters

Tools and materials

- Wool and the Gang Crazy Sexy Wool super chunky (super bulky) in
  - 1 x 200g (7oz) ball in Mineral Pink (231)
  - 1 x 200g (7oz) ball in Beige Blonde (229)
- 1 x 170g (6oz) ball of Lion Brand Wool-Ease Thick & Quick super chunky (super bulky) yarn in Starlight (308)
- 10mm (US15) knitting needles
- Scissors
- Tapestry needle

Finished size:
Coaster 1 – 13 x 11cm (5¼ x 4¼in)
Coaster 2 – 12 x 10.5cm (4¾ x 4¼in)
Coaster 3 – 14 x 12cm (5½ x 4¾in)

Tension:
Coasters 1 and 2 = 8 sts x 18 rows on 10mm (US15) needles
Coaster 3 = 7 sts x 16 rows on 10mm (US15) needles

Technique used:
Garter Stitch
(see page 20)

These knitted coasters are the perfect project for beginner knitters and provide a lovely table accessory for your morning coffee or tea. Coasters are a great way of adding colour and texture to your home, while providing something functional to protect your dining table.

This project can be explored using a range of three different yarn colours in a variety of combinations. For example, using one yarn colour or mixing yarn colours together to form interesting surface textures. This can be easily achieved using simple garter stitch.

with every stitch, knit and breathe

to make

teacup coaster 1: one yarn colour

1 Cast on 10 stitches (see pages 13–15) in pale pink.

2 Knit 16 rows in garter stitch (see page 20).

3 Begin to cast off your knitting (page 34) – knit 2 stitches and take the first stitch over the second stitch.

4 Cast off your knitting until you reach the last stitch on the needle.

5 Cut your yarn leaving a 10cm (4in) tail and take the tail of the yarn through the loop to fasten off.

6 Thread the tail of the yarn through the tapestry needle and weave it through the stitches at the back of the coaster. Weave the tail through the knitted stitches on the top edge (see page 40).

7 Repeat step 6 with any other loose ends. You have completed a knitted coaster.

1

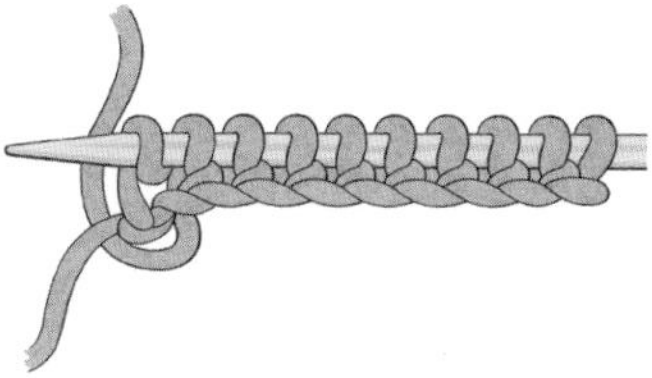

2

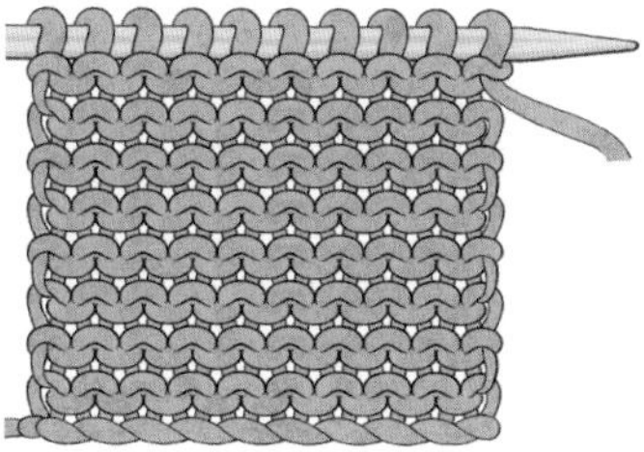

3

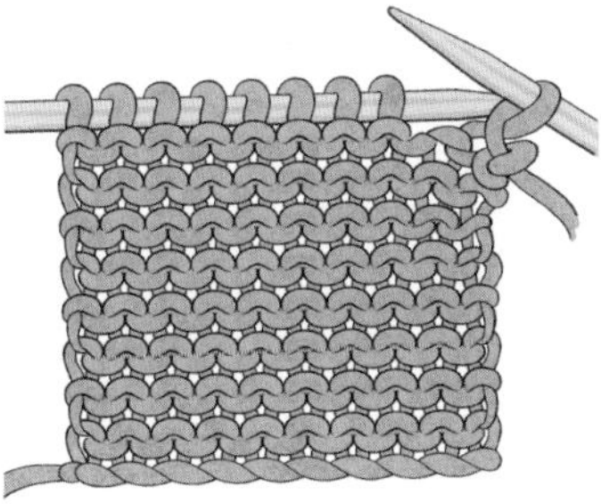

4

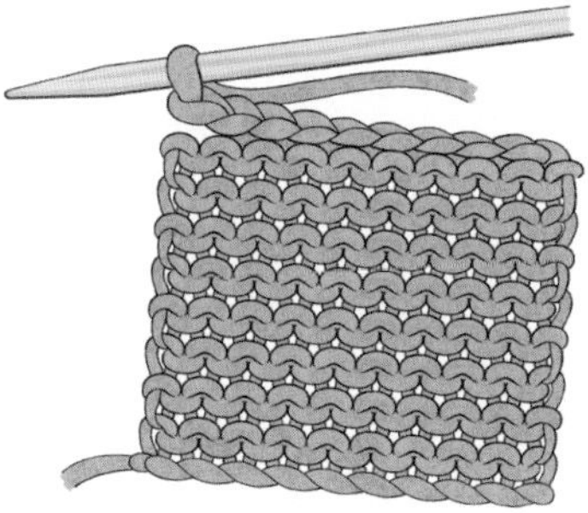

5

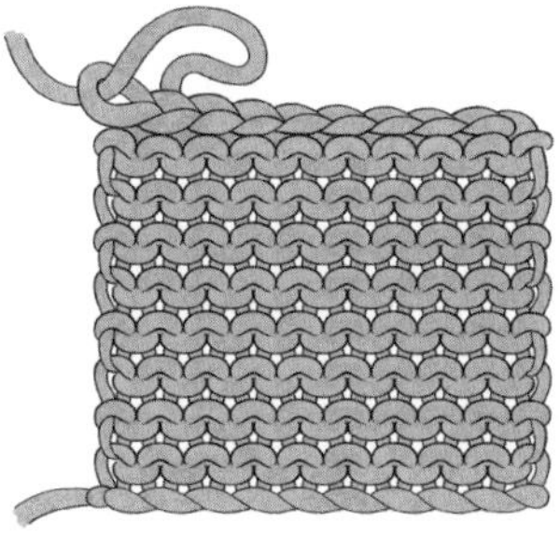

6

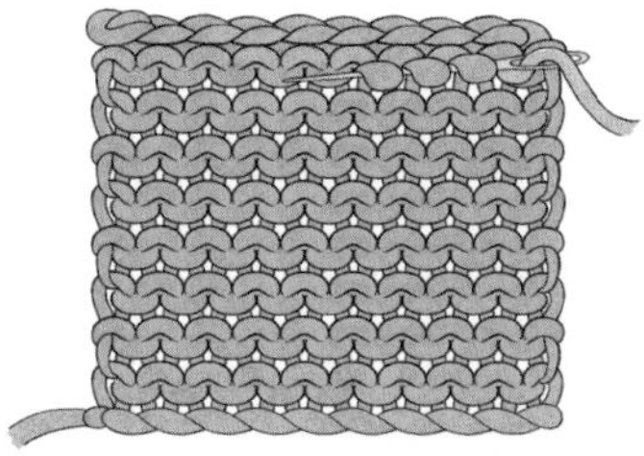

teacup coaster 2: two yarn colours

1 Cast on 10 stitches (see pages 13–15) in pale pink (the first yarn colour). Knit 8 rows in garter stitch (see page 20).

2 Change yarn colour to white (see page 32).

3 Knit one row with the new yarn colour. There should now be one row of white across the rows of pink.

4 Knit 8 more rows in garter stitch using white.

5 Begin to cast off your knitting (see page 34). Knit 2 stitches and take the first stitch over the second stitch. continue to cast off until you reach the last stitch on the needle. Cut the yarn leaving a tail of about 10cm (4in) and take the tail of the yarn through the loop to fasten off.

6 Thread the tail of the yarn through the tapestry needle and weave it through the stitches at the back of the coaster (see page 40).

7 Weave the tail end of the white yarn through the first row of white stitches at the back of the coaster (row 8).

8 Repeat steps 6 and 7 with any other loose yarn ends. You have completed a knitted coaster.

1

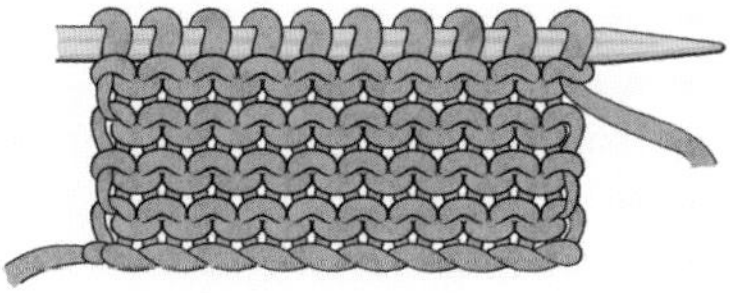

2

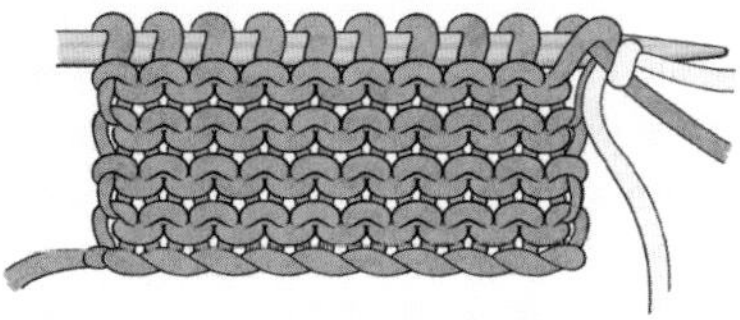

3

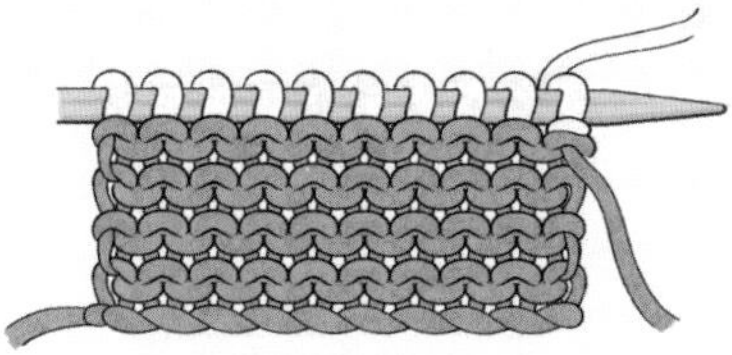

4

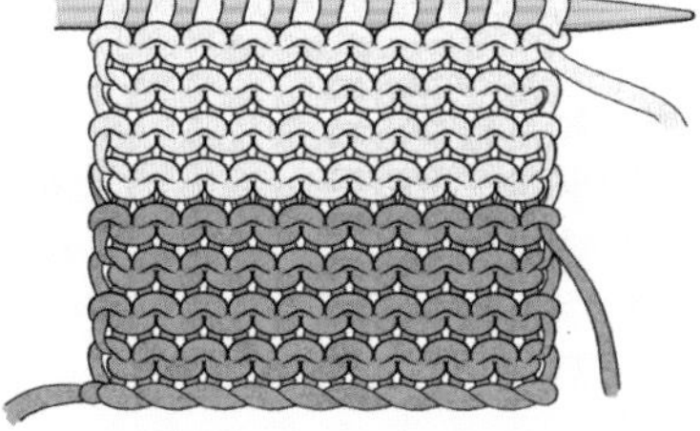

5

6

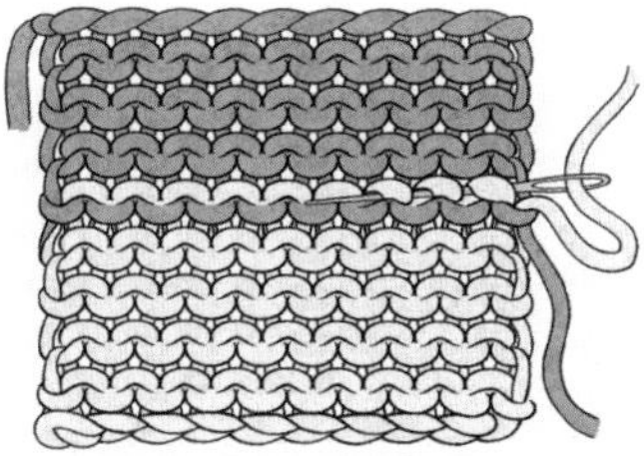

teacup coaster 3: two yarn colours held together

1 Holding beige and white together, make a slipknot on your LH needle (see page 12).

2 Cast on another 9 stitches using both yarns held together. You will have a total of 10 stitches on your needle. Knit 14 rows in garter stitch (see page 20).

3 Cast off your knitting using both yarns held together (see page 34) until you reach the last stitch on the needle.

4 Cut the yarn leaving a 10cm (4in) tail and take the tail through the loop to fasten off.

5 Thread the tail of the yarn through the tapestry needle and weave it through the stitches at the back of the coaster (see page 40).

6 Repeat step 5 with any other loose yarn ends. You now have a finished knitted coaster.

1

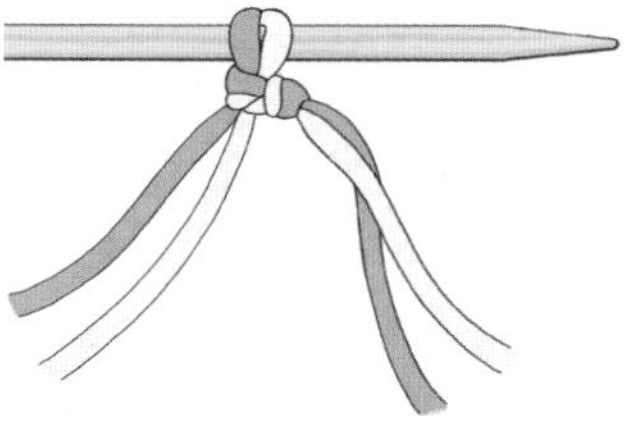

2

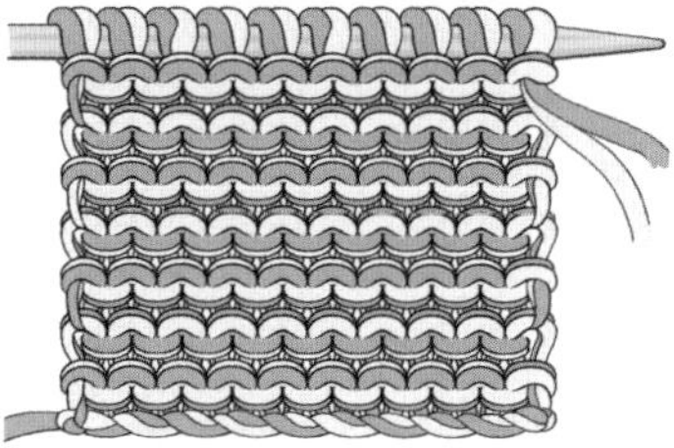

3

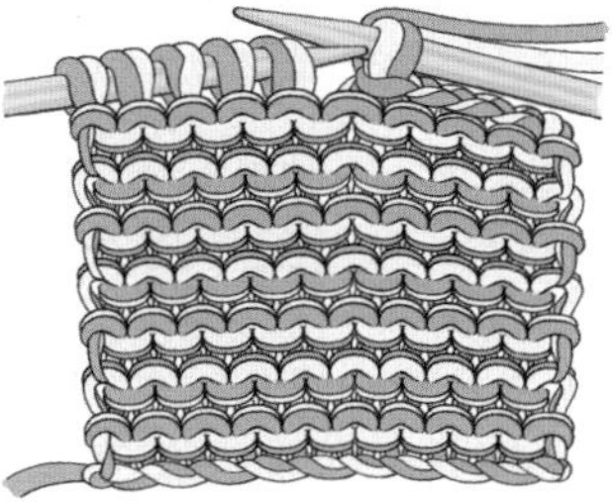

4

5

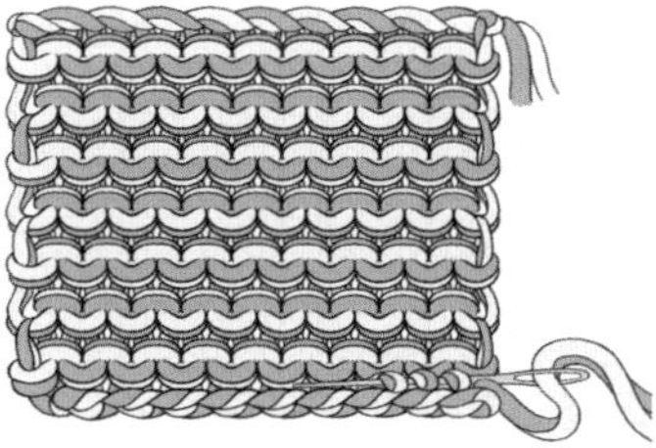

6

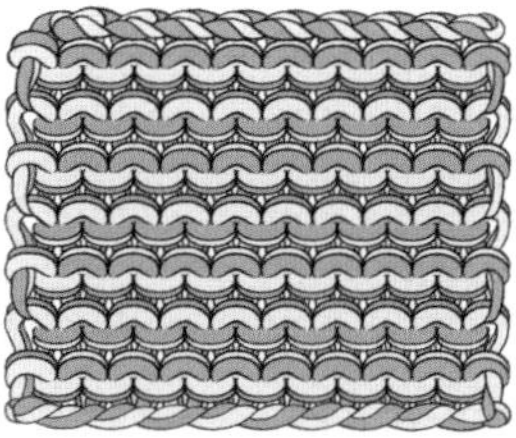

desk mat

A knitted desk mat is the perfect addition to your home workspace. Use it as a special zone in which to place your notebook and pens to help declutter your mind during the day.

You can use a combination of either wool or cotton yarns and experiment with different colourways to brighten up your workspace. The mat also has yarn fringing to add a sense of playfulness and texture to the design.

Tools and materials

- Lion Brand Wool-Ease Thick & Quick super chunky (super bulky) in
  - 1 x 170g (6oz) ball in Starlight (308)
  - 1 x 170g (6oz) ball in Claret (143)
- 10mm (US15) knitting needles
- Scissors
- Tapestry needle
- Piece of card, 20 x 12.5 cm (8 x 5in)
- Crochet hook

Finished size:
25 x 46cm (9¾ x 18in)

Tension:
7 sts x 13 rows = 10cm (4in) on 10mm (US15) needles

Technique used:
Garter Stitch (see page 20)

to make

1 Cast on 18 sts using cream (the first yarn colour) (see pages 13–15).

2 Knit 28 rows in garter stitch (see page 20).

3a Change to brown (the second yarn colour).

3b Tie the new yarn into a knot around the cream yarn tail (see page 32).

4a Knit one row with the new yarn colour. There should bow be one row of brown across the rows of cream.

4b Knit 27 more rows in garter stitch using brown.

5 When you reach row 56 cast off your knitting (see page 34).

6 Where you have changed/added your new yarn colour the work will have loose yarn ends. Weave these into your knitting using the tapestry needle (see page 40).

1

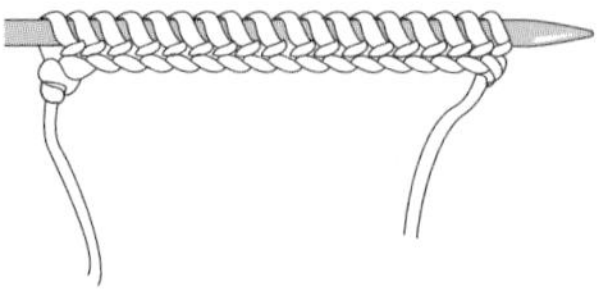

3b

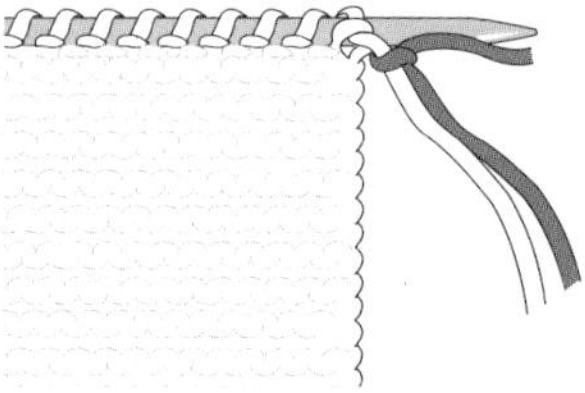

6

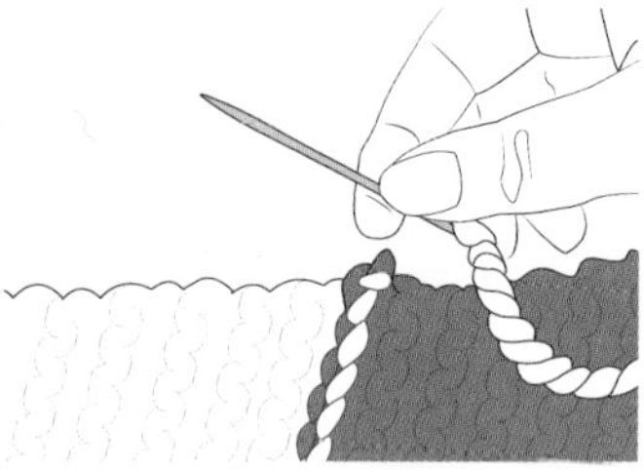

2

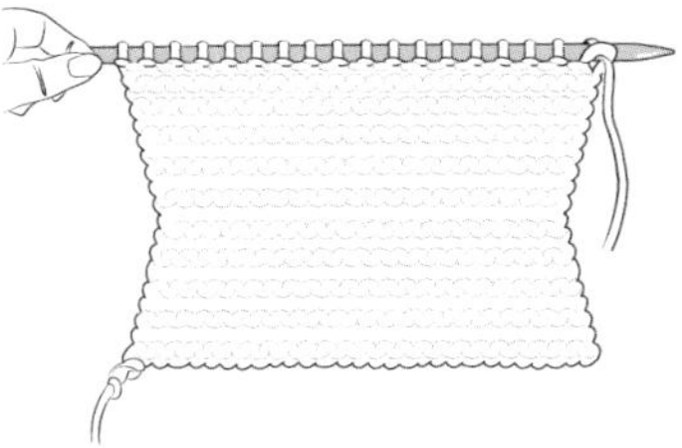

3a

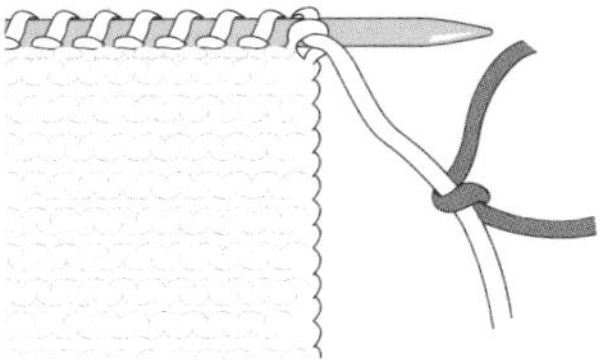

4a

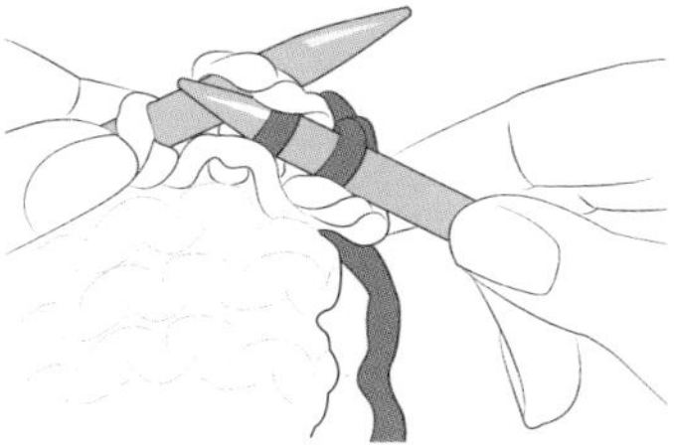

4b

adding a fringe

1 Cut out a 20 x 12.5cm (8 x 5in) piece of card. For each separate tail of the fringe you usually need at least two strands of yarn, so you will need to wind the yarn around the card enough times to make the number of strands you need. In this case there are 18 stitches in your knitting, so you need at least 36 strands (18 x 2).

2 Now cut through all the strands along one edge of the card.

3 Separate out two strands of fringing, then insert the crochet hook into a stitch of the cast-on edge of the desk mat. Now place the folded loop of fringing onto the crochet hook.

4 Pull the loop of fringing yarn through the knitted stitch to the front.

5 Hook the tails of your fringe with the crochet hook and pull them through the loop of the fringe yarn. Pull on the tails to tighten the knot.

6 Repeat for each stitch along the edge of the desk mat. You have now created a fringe!

7 When you have finished attaching the fringing to one side of your desk mat repeat on the other side to complete the design.

8 When all fringing has been attached to the edges of the mat, lay all of the work flat and trim the fringing to the same length on both sides.

today is filled with endless possibilities

1

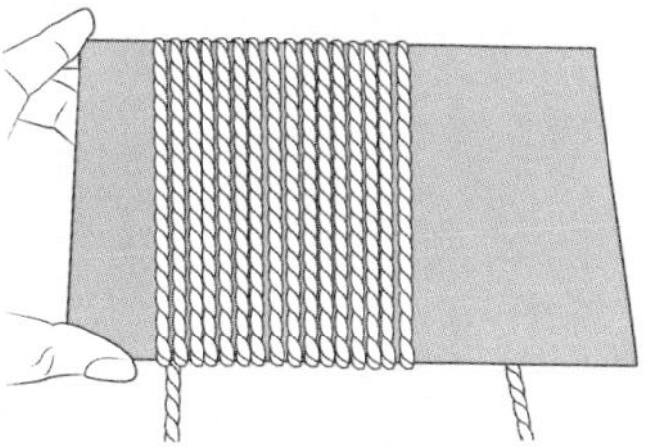

2

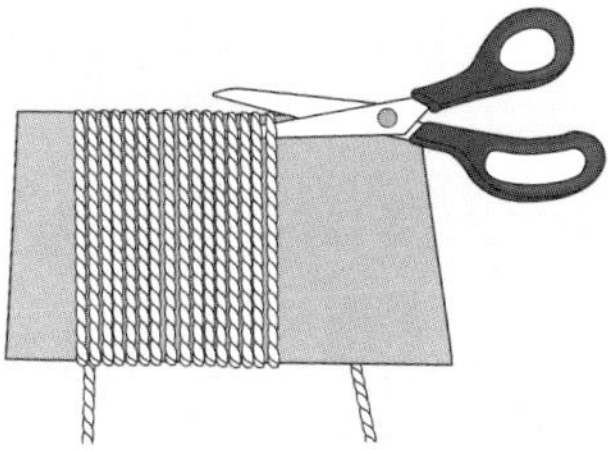

3

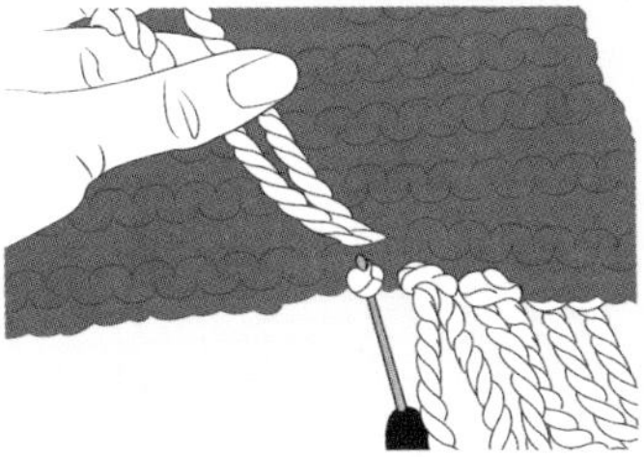

4

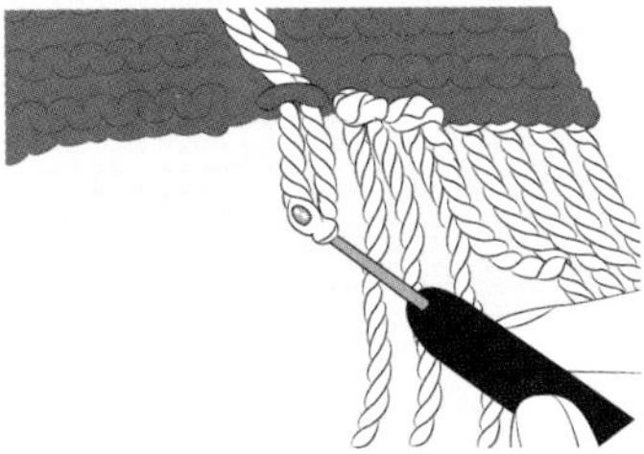

5

8

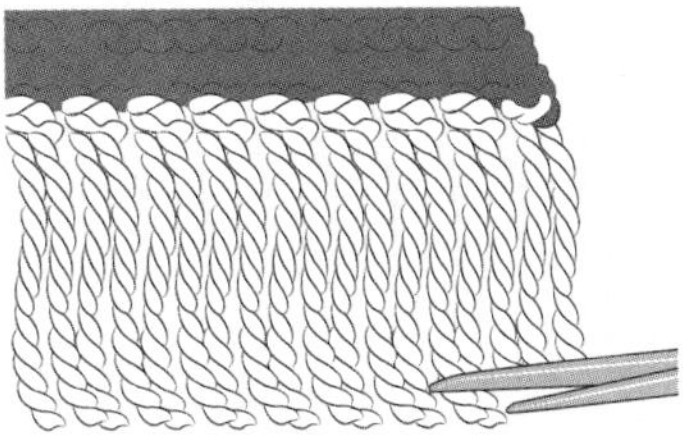

bathroom mat

Tools and materials

- Cascade Sarasosta chunky (bulky) yarn:
  - 2 x 200g (7oz) balls in Chincilla (242)
  - 2 x 200g (7oz) balls in White (224)
- 8mm (US11) knitting needles
- Scissors
- Tapestry needle

Finished size:
Approx. 50 x 70cm
(19¾ x 27½in)

Tension:
10 sts x 13 rows = 10cm (4in) on 8mm (US11) needles

Technique used:
Stocking stitch
(see page 21)

Stepping onto a cozy and soft knitted bathmat as you brush your teeth, or after you've had a long, relaxing soak in the bath, is just heavenly; your feet will thank you. This knitted bath mat is a great addition to any bathroom: place it next to your bath, ready to be used, or in the middle of the room to add texture to the overall look.

Use a combination of thick wool or cotton yarn colours or try using just one soothing colour to induce a calm and cozy atmosphere.

to make

1 Cast on 46 stitches (see pages 13–15) using both yarn colours held together.

2 Knit 91 rows in stocking stitch (see page 21).

3 Cast off your knitting (see page 34) and weave in any loose ends using a tapestry needle (see page 40).

my creativity is boundless and flows effortlessly

1

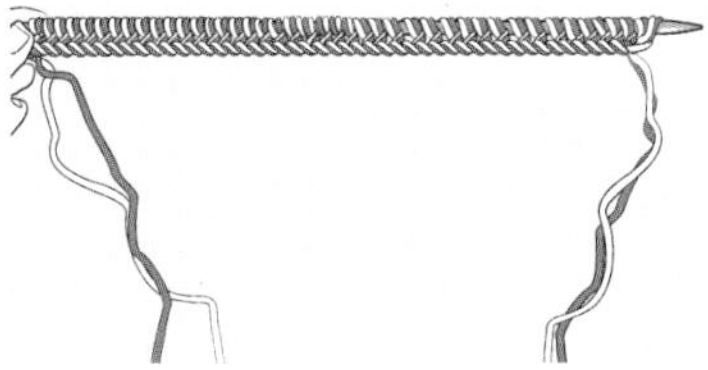

2

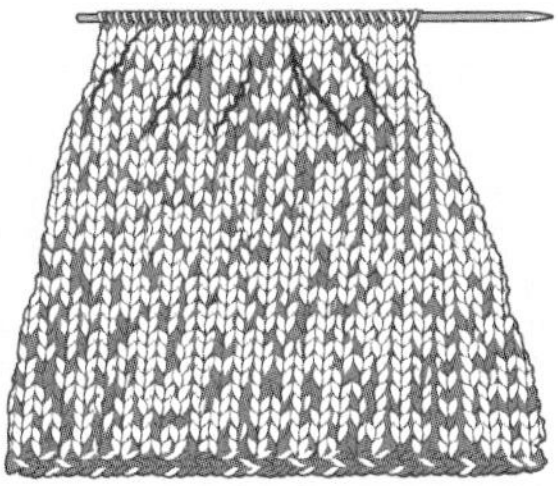

3

striped bathroom mat

Tools and materials

- Cascade Sarasosta chunky (bulky) yarn:
  - 2 x 200g (7oz) balls in Chincilla (242)
  - 2 x 200g (7oz) balls in Celadon (240)
  - 2 x 200g (7oz) balls in White (224)
- 8mm (US11) knitting needles
- Scissors
- Tapestry needle

Finished size:
Approx. 50 x 75cm
(19¾ x 29½in)

Tension:
10 sts x 13 rows
= 10cm (4in) on 8mm
(US11) needles

Technique used:
Stocking Stitch
(see page 21)

For this bathmat, choose a combination of soothing yarn colours that will complement your bathroom. It will add to the sense of relaxation, especially when you have a moment of peace away from all the noise.

to make

1 Cast on 46 stitches (see pages 13–15) using two strands of Chincilla (beige) held together.

2 Knit 13 rows in stocking stitch (see page 21) with two strands held together.

3 Change colour to Celadon (mint green) (see page 32). Knit 6 rows in stocking stitch with two strands held together.

4 Change colour to two strands of White. Knit 6 rows in stocking stitch with two strands held together. Change yarn colour to two strands of beige.

5 Repeat steps 2–4 three more times until you reach row 100. You will end with a white stripe and two strands of beige ready to use.

6 Knit 13 rows in stocking stitch with two strands of beige held together.

7 Cast off your knitting (see page 34) and weave in any loose ends using the tapestry needle (see page 40).

repeat the word 'love' out loud as you place each stitch on the needle

1

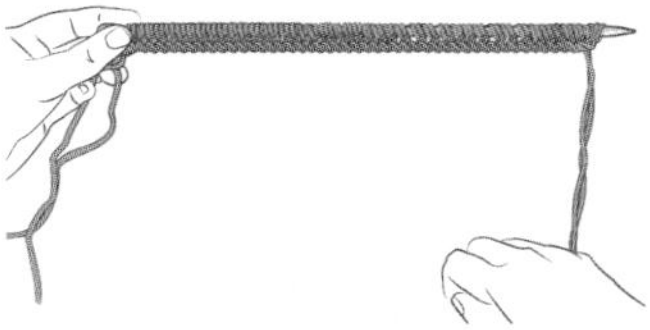

2

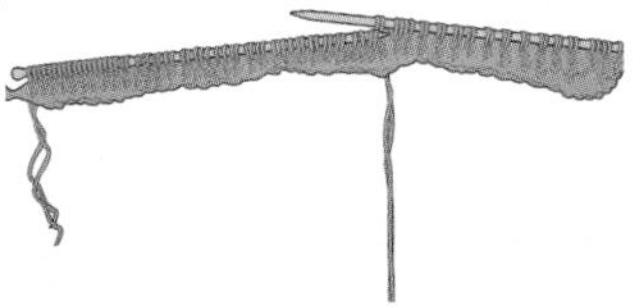

3

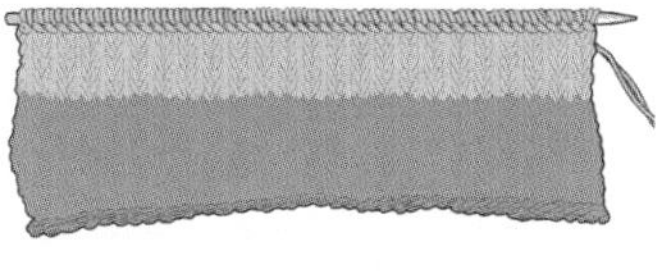

4

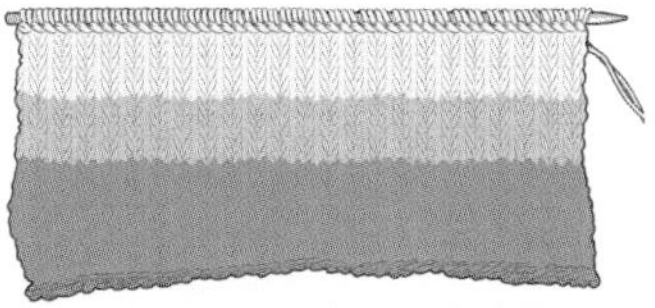

5

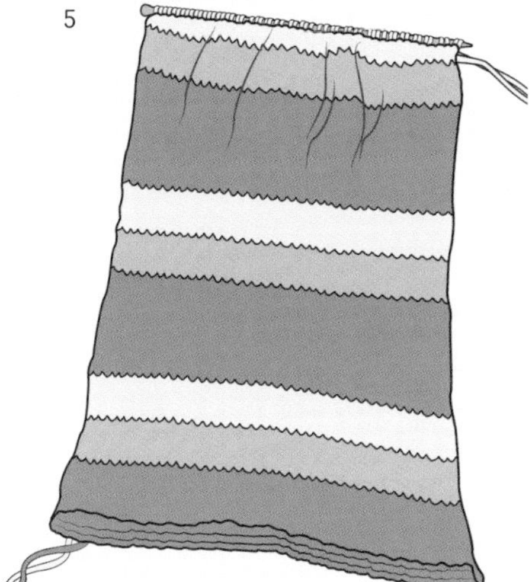

6

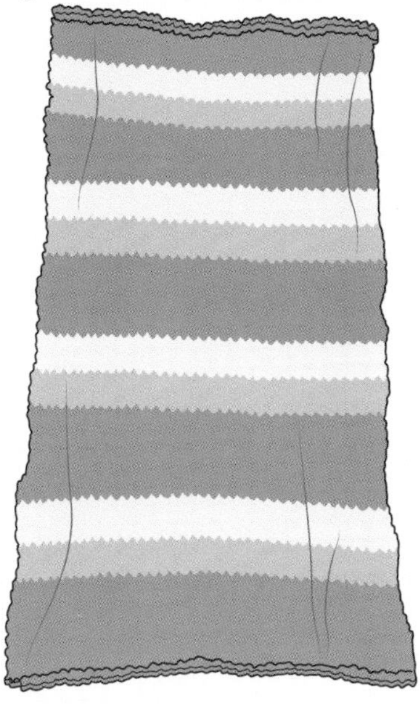

dish cloths

Cotton and linen is the go-to yarn for knitted dishcloths because it is durable and washable at high temperatures. It's likely that you'll have some cotton or Linen yarn in your stash already. These dishcloths are intricately made and soft to the touch and they'll glide beautifully on the countertops. Choose a combination of colour tones that fits uniquely into your kitchen space.

Tools and materials

- Rowan Creative Linen DK (light worsted) yarn:
  - 1 x 100g (3½oz) ball in Pumpkin (651)
  - 1 x 100g (3½oz) ball in Straw (622)
- 4.5mm (US7) knitting needles
- Scissors
- Tapestry needle

Finished size:
20 x 20cm (8 x 8in)

Tension:
21 sts X 28 rows = 10cm (4in) on 4.5mm (US7) needles

Technique used:
1 x 1 Rib Stitch
(see page 30)

to make

1 Cast on 42 stitches (see pages 13–15).

2 Knit for 41 rows knit in 1 x 1 rib stitch (see page 30).

3 Cast off your knitting (see page 34) and weave in any loose yarn ends using the tapestry needle (see page 40).

embrace the beauty of the handmade.

1

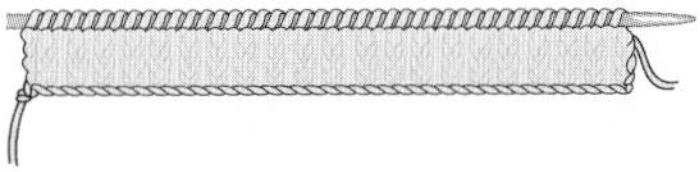

2

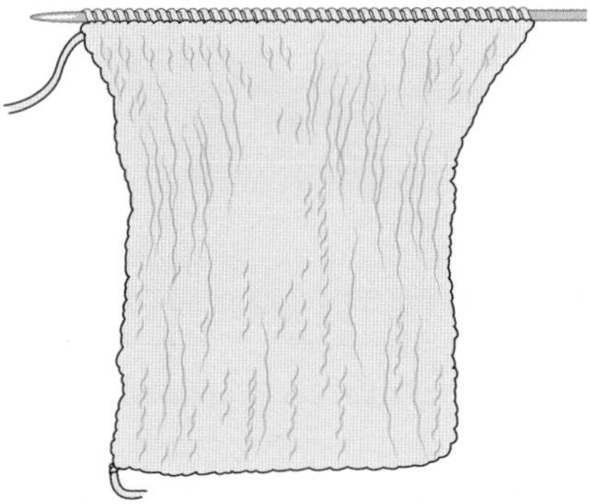

3

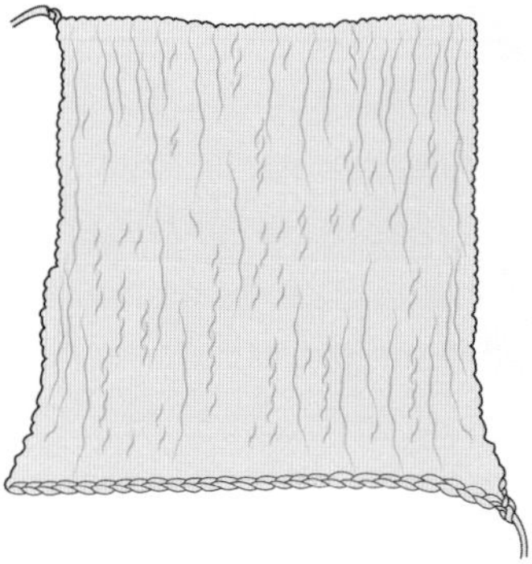

knitted blanket

Tools and materials

- Rowan Big Wool super chunky (super bulky) yarn:
  - 2 x 100g (3½oz) balls in Biscotti (082)
  - 2 x 100g (3½oz) balls in Golden Olive (088)
  - 2 x 100g (3½oz) balls in Linen (048)
  - 2 x 100g (3½oz) balls in Vert (054)
- 12mm (US17) circular knitting needles
- Scissors
- Tapestry needle

Finished size:
80 x 160cm
(31½ x 70in)

Tension:
8 sts x 10 rows
= 10cm (4in) on 12mm
(US17) needles

Technique used:
Garter Stitch
(see page 20)

Imagine perching on your sofa in your favourite spot, and then imagine you have something soft, unique and homemade to throw over yourself to make yourself feel even more comfortable! This large knitted blanket is that unique, homemade something – get ready for extra comfort and relaxation.

This stocking stitch blanket uses super soft, chunky merino wool and is knitted in a pleasing range of colours to create a colour-block-stripe effect for maximum style and coziness. This pattern also introduces the technique of slipping stitches. To slip a stitch is to pass it from one needle to another without knitting it. Some knitting patterns and techniques may require you to either slip stitches knitwise or purlwise. The way you slip a stitch alters the final outcome. Here we do it purlwise.

relax with the rhythm of the stitches

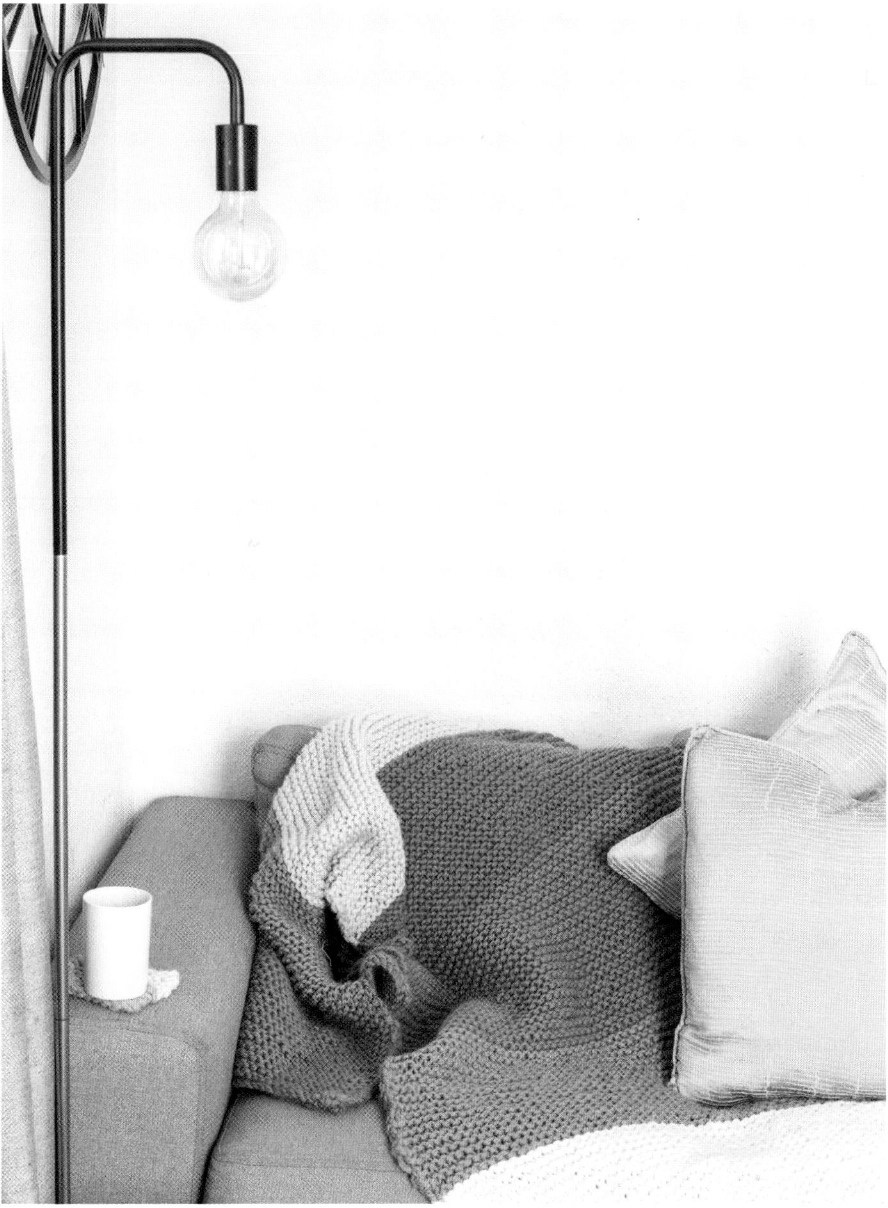

to make

1 Cast on 75 stitches in Biscotti (brown) (see pages 13–15). Before you knit each row slip the first stitch purlwise. To do this, insert the right-hand needle into the first stitch on the left-hand needle as if to purl from the back of the stitch to the front.

2 Slip the stitch off the left-hand needle, onto the right-hand needle then continue knitting the rest of the stitches on the row.

3 Knit 20 rows in garter stitch (see page 20) in brown, slip the first stitch purlwise each time, to make neat edges.

4 Change colour to Golden Olive (olive) (see page 32) then knit 20 rows.

5 Change colour to Linen (cream) then knit 20 rows.

6 Change colour to Vert (green) then knit 20 rows.

7 Change colour to brown then knit 20 rows.

8 Change colour to olive then knit 20 rows.

9 Change colour to cream then knit 20 rows.

10 Cast off your knitting (see page 34) and weave in any loose ends using the tapestry needle (see page 40).

1

4

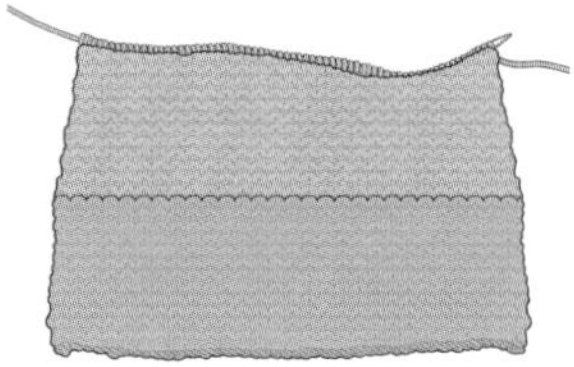

7

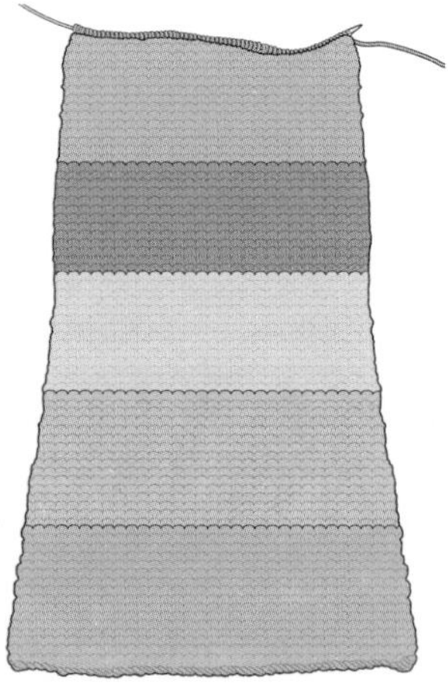

2

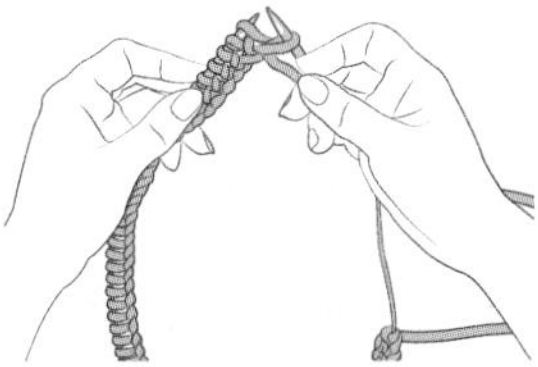

3

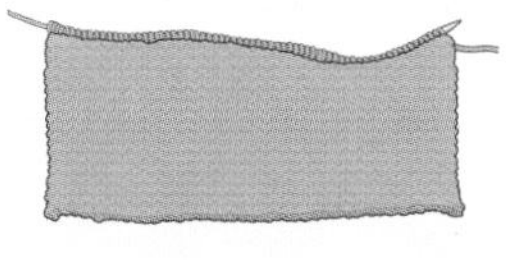

5

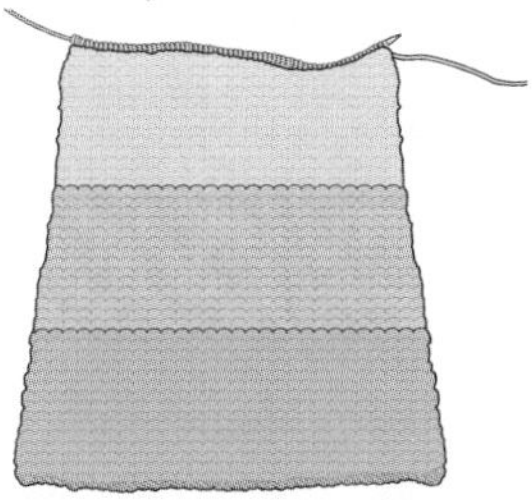

6

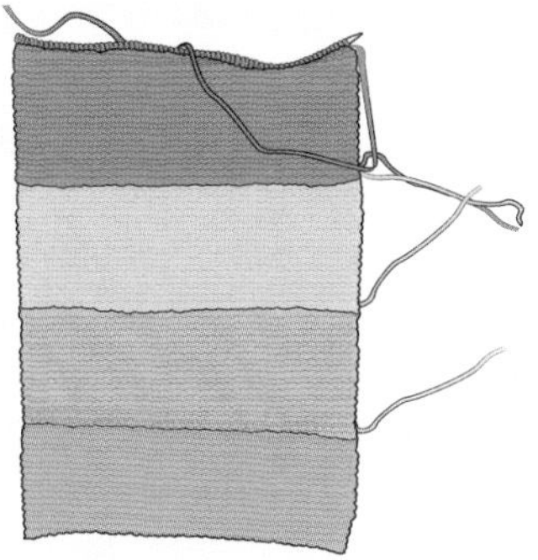

8

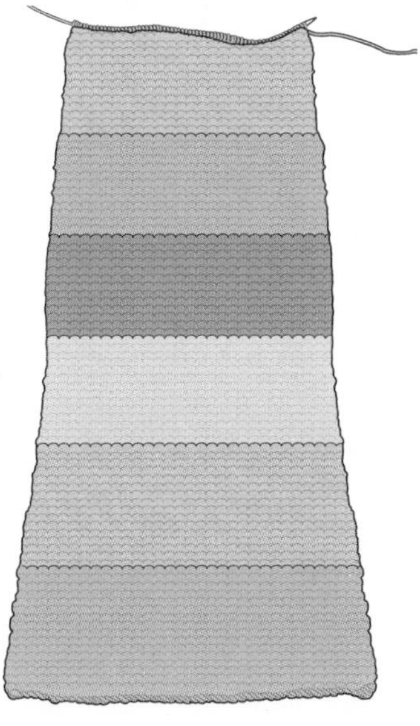

9

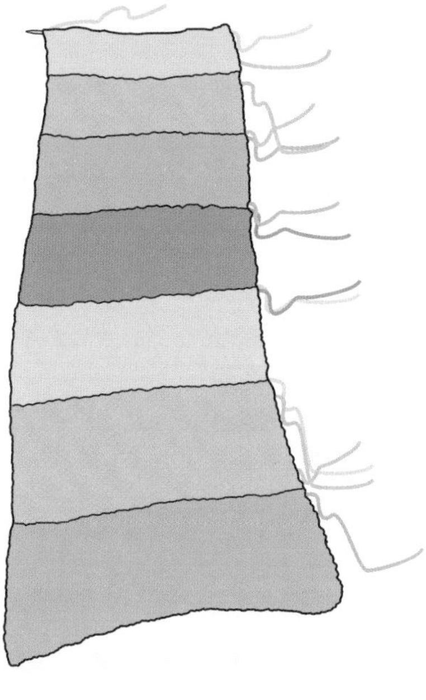

textured wall hanging

Tools and materials

- 1 x 100g (3½oz) ball of Rowan Big Wool super chunky (super bulky) yarn in Golden Olive (088)
- 1 x 100g (3½oz) ball of Cascade Canata aran (worsted) yarn in Gold (06)
- Cascade Magnum Super Chunky (super bulky) yarn in:
  - 1 x 250 (8¾oz) ball in Ecru (10)
  - 1 x 250 (8¾oz) ball in Doeskin Heather (8012)
  - 1 x 250 (8¾oz) ball in Sphere (9565)
- 1 x 100g (3½oz) ball of Knitcraft Leader of the Pac aran (worsted) yarn in Green Teal
- 12mm (US17) bamboo knitting needles
- Scissors
- Tapestry needle
- 2 x 30cm (11¾in) bamboo dowel rods or 1 100cm (39¼in) dowel rod

Finished size:
74 x 56cm (29¼ x 22in).
Fringe = 10cm (4in)

Techniques used:
Garter Stitch
(see page 20)

Here's an opportunity to fill your blank walls with something unique and interesting: a talking point with texture and soft colour tones, that is sure to enhance the comforts of your home.

A combination of thick, soft wool yarns and thinner linen yarns is used in this garter stitch wall hanging to create a decorative piece alive with texture and contrast. You can also try mixing colours to form intriguing patterns. The possibilities are endless.

notice the detail

to make

1 Cast on 45 stitches (see pages 13–15). Start with the colour that will be at the bottom of the wall hanging (keep in mind that this is where the fringing will be attached), in this case Sphere (light blue).

2 Knit 20 rows in garter stitch (see page 20).

3 Change colour to Gold (see page 32) then knit 5 rows. The gold yarn is a lot thinner than the blue yarn, so it will give a textured 'holey' effect.

4 Change colour to Ecru (cream) and hold the two yarns together and knit 1 row in garter stitch.

5 Cut off the gold yarn and knit for 20 rows with the cream yarn.

6 Change colour to the Doeskin Heather (grey) mohair yarn.

7 Knit 3 rows with cream and grey held together – creating a marbled, striped effect.

8 Cut off the cream yarn and knit 8 rows in grey.

1

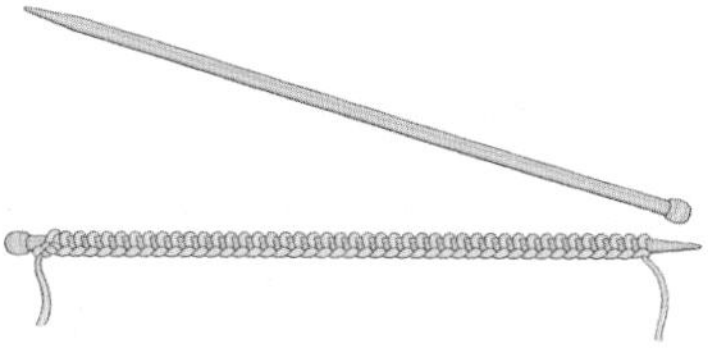

2

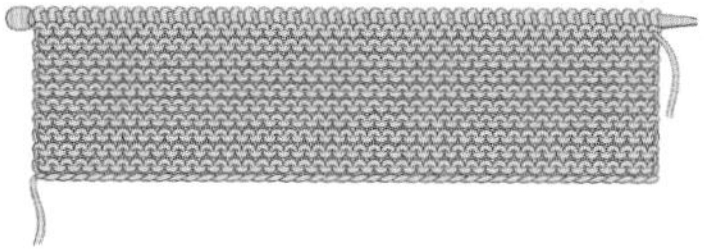

4

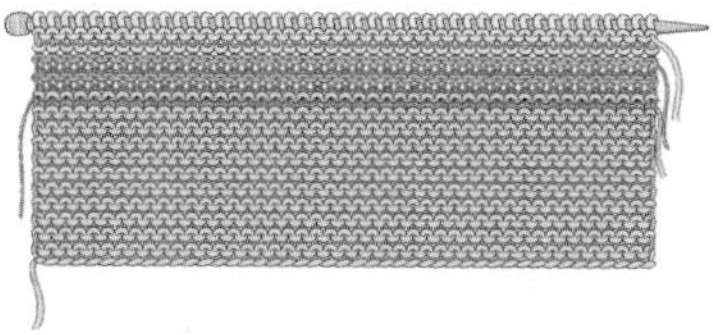

5

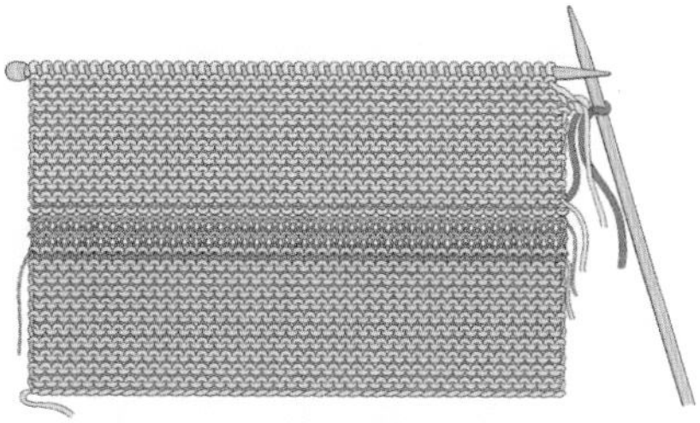

7

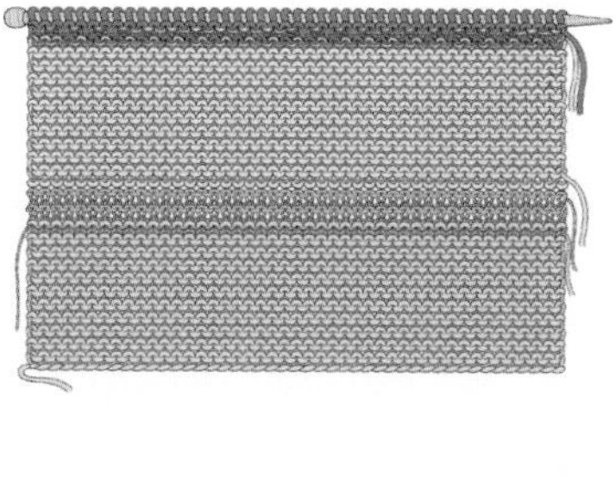

8

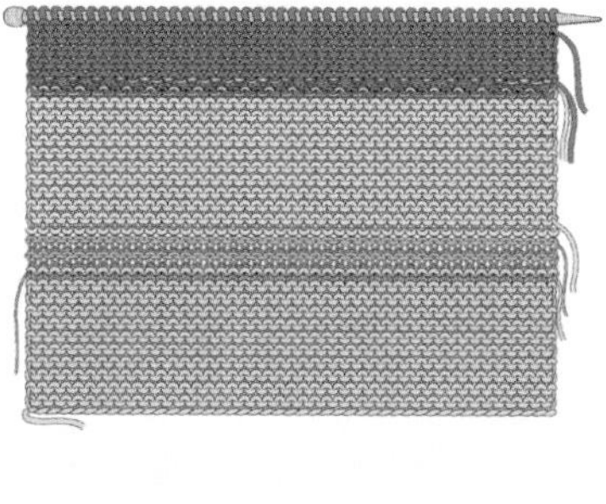

9

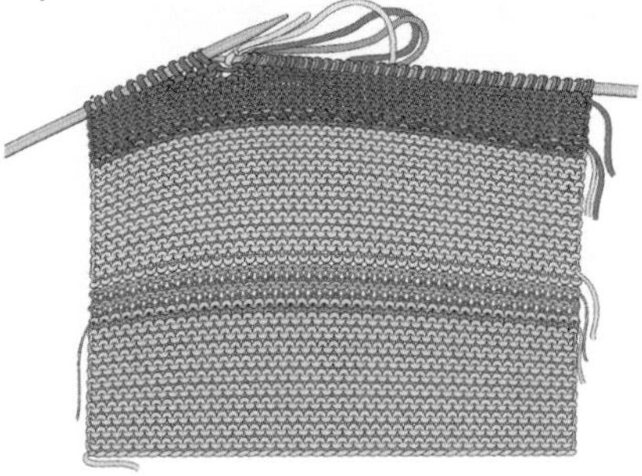

10

11

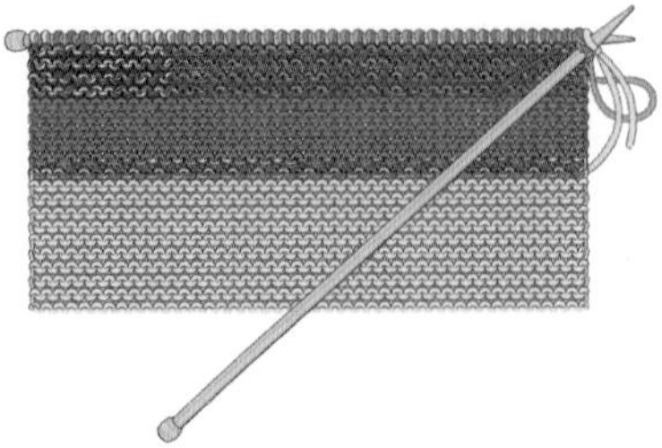

13

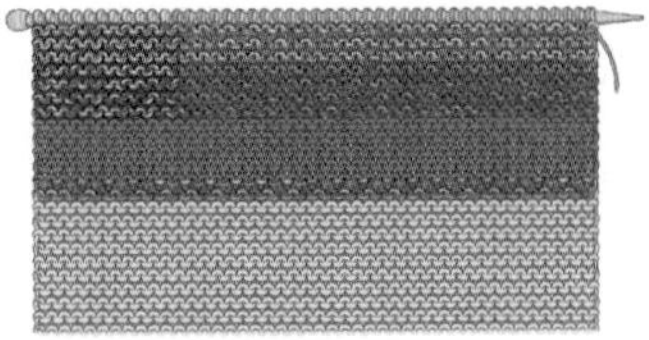

9 Change colour to olive and knit 8 rows held together with the grey and olive yarns.

10 Next row: Knit 33 stitches with grey and olive yarns held together, join in the cream yarn and knit the last 12 stitches with grey, olive and cream yarns held together.
Next row: Knit the first 12 sts with grey, olive and cream yarns held together, drop the cream yarn and knit the last 33 stitches with grey and olive yarns held together.
These 2 rows should create a patchwork of three colours on the left side of the wall hanging and two colours on the right side.
Knit 6 rows more in this patchwork pattern.

11 Cut off the grey and join in the light blue yarn. Again knit the first 12 stitches with light blue, olive and cream yarns held together.

12 Cut off the cream yarn and knit the last 33 stitches with light blue and olive yarn together. Repeat this pattern for the next 5 rows.

13 Cut off the light blue yarn and knit 3 rows with olive yarn.

14

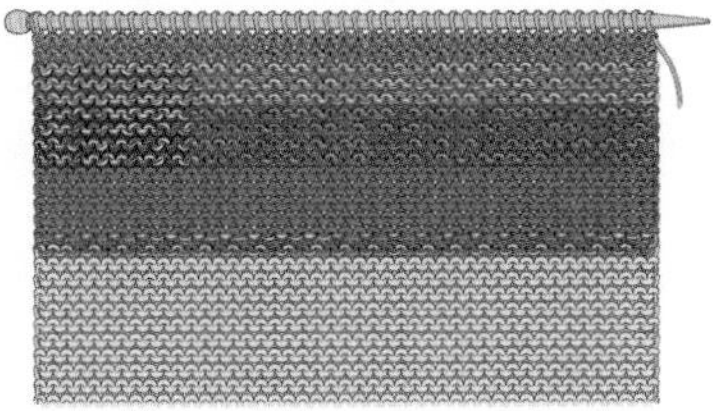

15

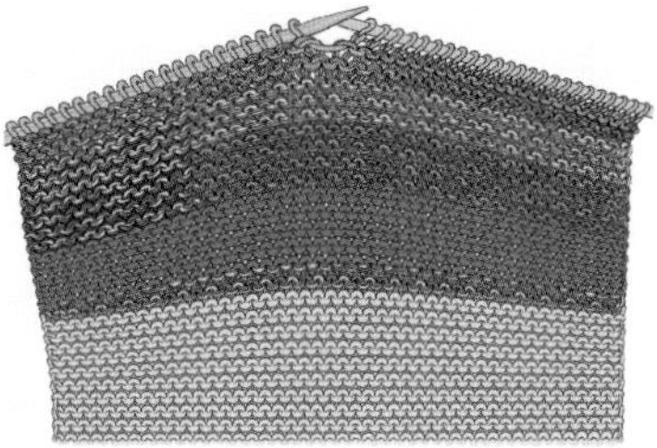

17

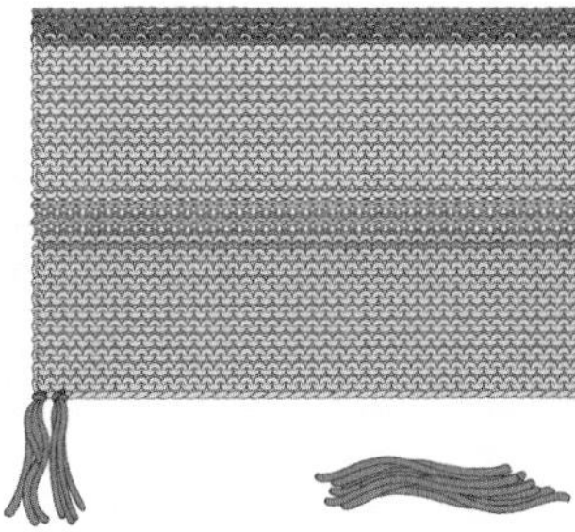

18

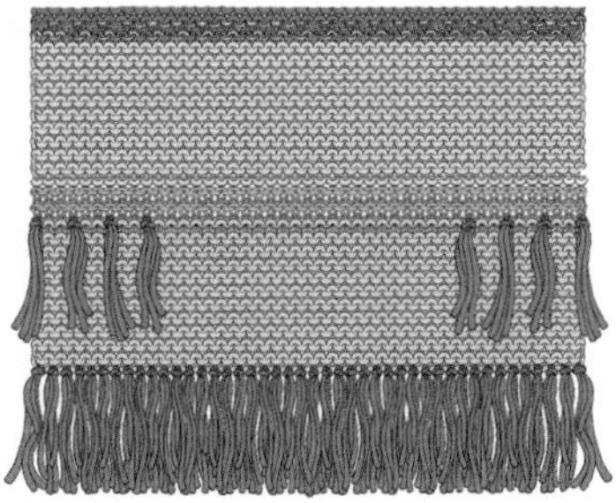

14 Change colour to gold and knit 4 rows with olive and gold yarns held together.

15 Cut off the olive yarn. If you're using two shorter dowels, replace the needle without the stitches with a dowel and knit 2 rows with the gold yarn, using one dowel and one knitting needle. If you're using a single longer dowel, continue to use both needles to the end of the pattern.

16 Knit 1 row with both shorter dowel rods, ending in the centre of the row so the knitting is ready on the dowels for hanging. Weave in any loose ends using the tapestry needle (see page 40).

17 Cut the Green Teal yarn into 10cm (4in) strands and pair them up to tie together. Attach the two strands of yarn to every stitch of the bottom row of the hanging (see page 114 for more information on fringing). Attach as many strands of fringing as you need to fill the space.

18 Attach 3 pieces of fringing at each side of the gold yarn (21 rows from the bottom upwards). If you're using a single, longer dowel rod, transfer the stitches onto it once the hanging is complete.

plant pot cozies

Taking care of plants doesn't have to be a chore, instead it can be something to look forward to, especially when you can make a beautiful cozy for each pot or vase. Making plant cozies is an easy way to add pops of colour to your plant collection and home.

A plant pot cozy's function is to look good while still allowing the plant to take centre stage. Simple and straightforward to make, they will bring joy to your home for years to come!

everything you want is out there waiting for you. everything you want also wants you

to make

large plant pot cozy

Tools and materials

- 1 x 200g (7oz) ball of Cascade Sarasosta chunky (bulky) yarn in Chinchilla (242)
- 1 x 100g (3½oz) ball of Cascade Andean Dream aran (worsted) yarn in Aqua Haze (12)
- 6mm (US10) knitting needles
- Scissors
- Tapestry needle

Finished size:
39 x 12.5cm (15¼ x 4in)

Tension:
14–16 sts = 10cm (4in) in Sarasota Chunky on 6mm (US10) knitting needles
18–20 sts = 10cm (4in) in Andean Dream on 6mm (US10) knitting needles

Technique used:
Garter Ridge Stitch (see page 26)

1 Cast on 47 stitches (see pages 13–15) in Chincilla (beige).

2 Begin with the garter ridge stitch pattern (see page 26):
Row 1: (RS) Knit.
Row 2: Purl.
Row 3: Knit.
Row 4: Knit.

3 Repeat step 2.

4 Change yarn colour to Aqua Haze (blue). Repeat step 2 five times until you reach row 28.

5 Continue in blue.
Row 1: Knit.
Row 2: Purl.

6 Change yarn colour to beige.
Row 1: Knit.
Row 2: Purl.

7 Cast off your knitting (see page 34) and weave in any loose ends using the tapestry needle (see page 40). Align the two sides together with the RS facing up. Use mattress stitch to join the two edges together (see page 36).

1

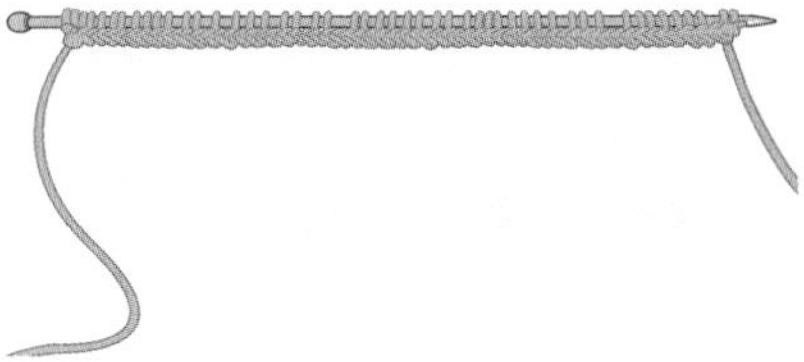

3

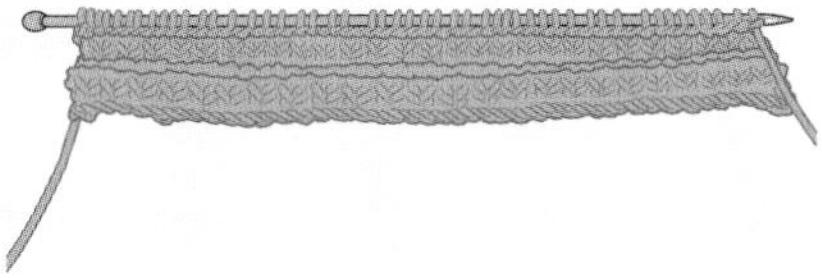

4

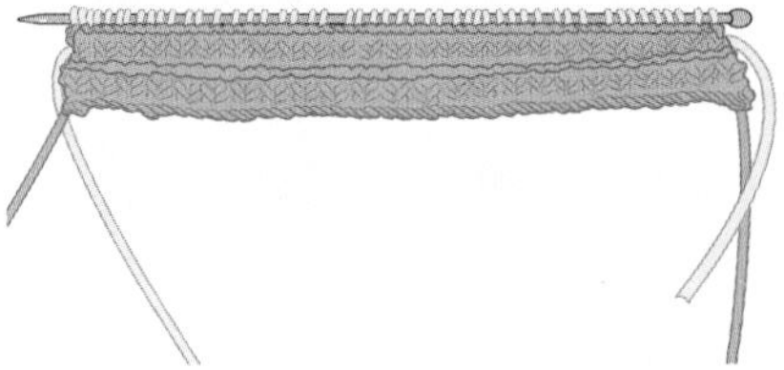

5

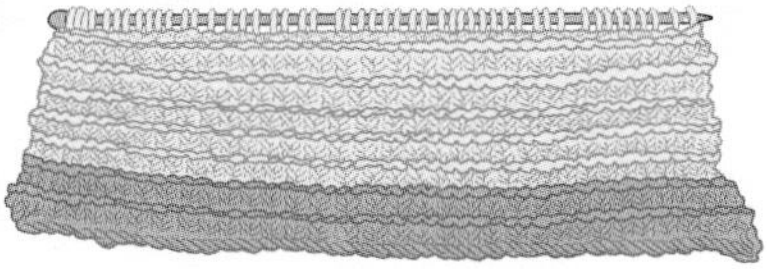

6

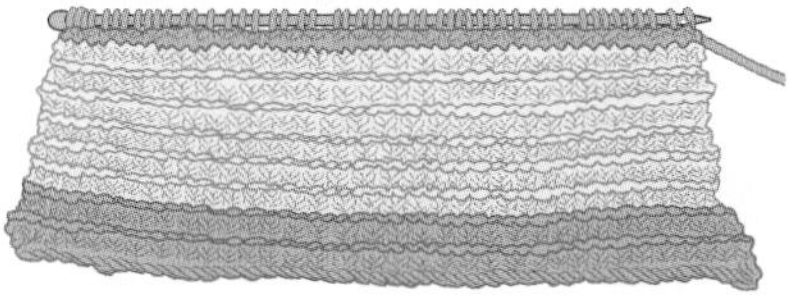

7

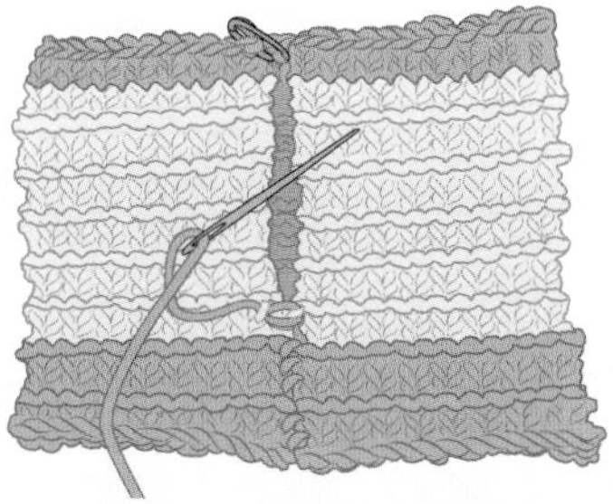

to make

small plant pot cozy

Tools and materials

- 1 x 100g (3½oz) ball of Cascade Cantata aran (worsted) yarn in Gold (06)
- 5mm (US8) knitting needles
- Tapestry needle
- Scissors

Finished size:
27 x 8cm (10½ x 3⅛in)

Tension:
18 sts = 10cm (4in) on 5mm (US8) needles

Technique used:
Large Garter Ridge Stitch (see page 28)

1 Cast on 39 stitches (see pages 13–15).

2 Continue with the large garter ridge stitch pattern (see page 28).
Row 1: (RS) Knit.
Row 2: Purl.
Row 3: Knit.
Row 4: Purl.
Rows 5–8: Purl.
Row 9: Knit.
Row 10: Purl.
Row 11: Knit.
Row 12: Purl.

3 Repeat rows 1 to 4.

4 Row 17: Knit.
Row 18: Purl.

5 Cast off your knitting (see page 34) and weave in any loose ends using the tapestry needle (see page 40).

6 Bring the two side edges together with RS facing up. Use mattress stitch to join the two side edges together (see page 36).

2

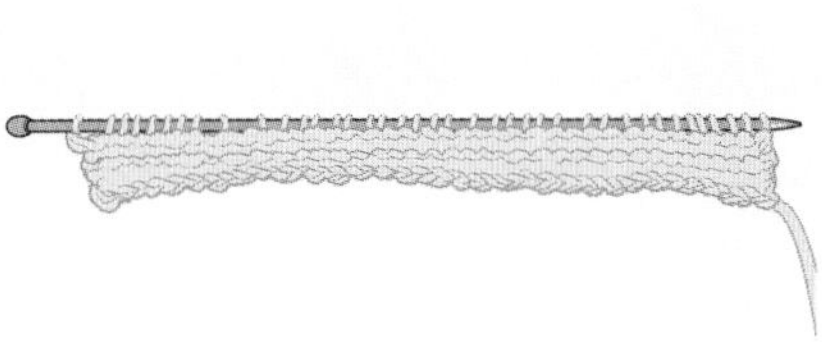

3

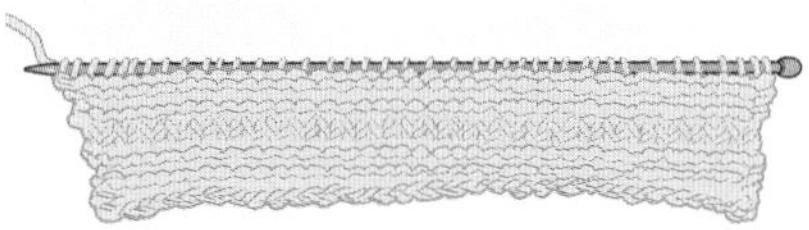

4

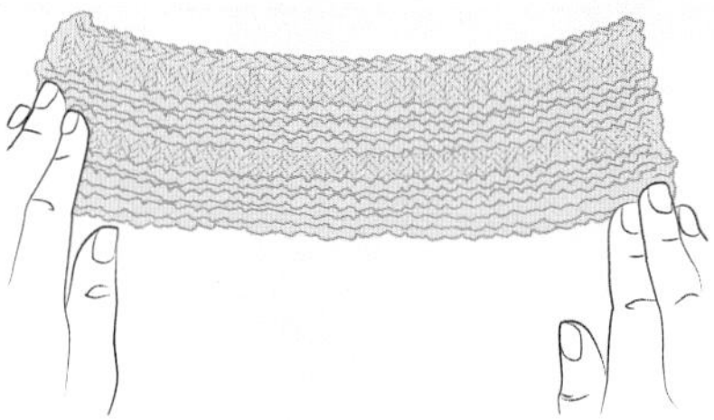

6

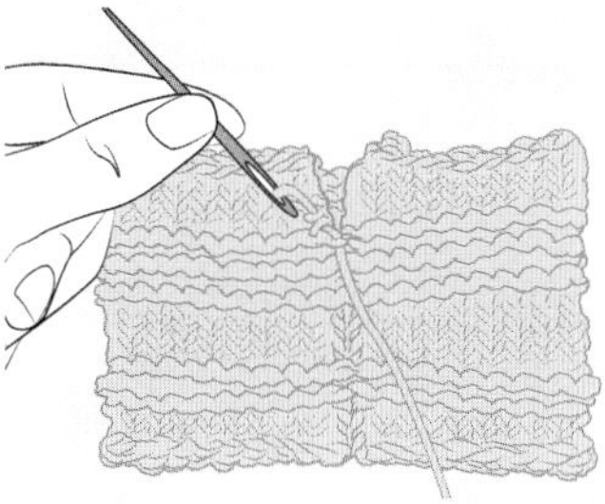

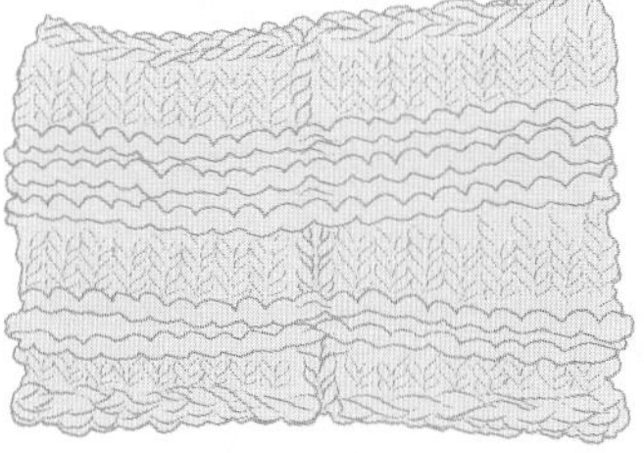

pom-pom Christmas wreath

Tools and materials

- Cascade Magnum Tweed super chunky (super bulky) yarn:
  - 1 x 250g (8¾oz) ball in Olive Oil (09)
  - 1 x 250g (8¾oz) ball in Ecru (07)
- Knitcraft Cotton Blend Plain DK yarn:
  - 1 x 100g (3½oz) ball in red
  - 1 x 100g (3½oz) ball in white
- 1 x 100g (3½oz) ball of Cascade Lana Grande super chunky (super bulky) yarn in Sienna (6029)
- 30cm (12in) polystyrene wreath
- 90cm x 50cm (35½ x 19½in) of forest green satin fabric
- Glue gun (optional)
- 1 x 9cm (3½in) pom-pom maker
- 1 x 5.5cm (2¼in) pom-pom maker
- Scissors

Finished size:
30cm (12in) diameter

T'is the season to be jolly! As the year draws to a close, there will be lots of time for cozy and warm reflections while making this celebration wreath. Each of the pom-poms can be made in different yarns or in different colours and arranged in endless combinations to reflect your own unique style.

Whether you cover the wreath totally with pom-poms or use some fabric to cover half of it, this is a crafty project that can be enjoyed by all the family and given as a gift to your neighbour or a friend. Either way, enjoy those moments of creative expression.

craft fills my soul, it is the vehicle
for expressing my vision

to make

1a

1b

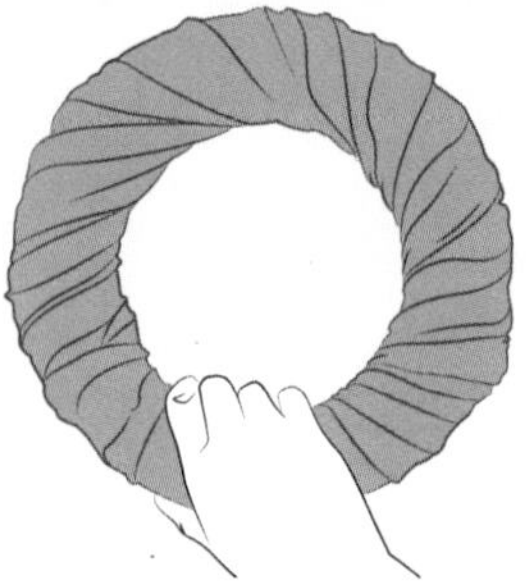

2

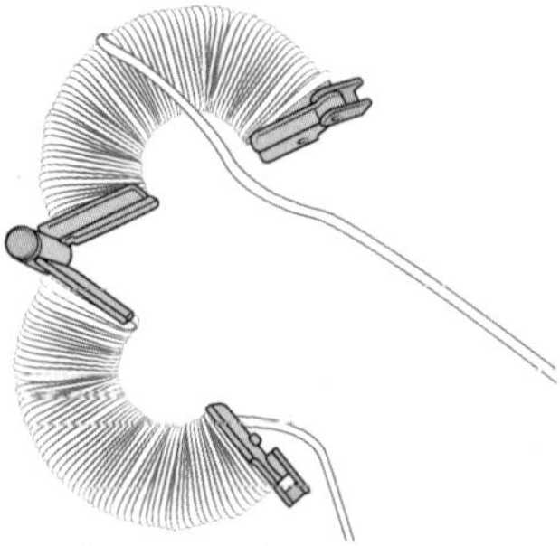

3

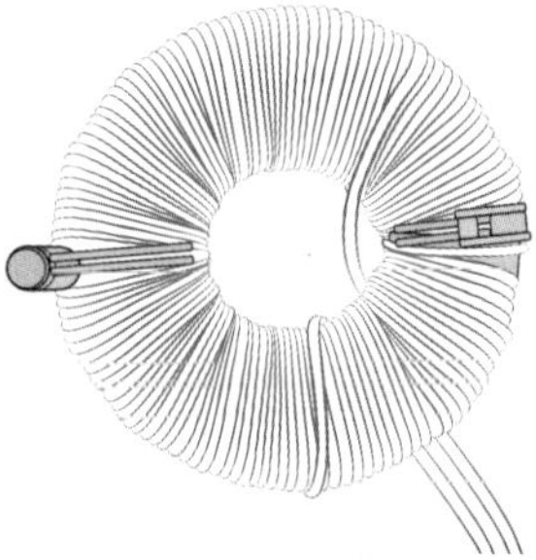

1a Use the satin fabric to cover the wreath, wrapping it around through the middle until it's completely covered.

1b Secure the fabric at the back using the glue gun or by wrapping the fabric very tightly into a secure knot at the back.

2 Take a pom-pom maker and your choice of yarn and wrap it around the pom-pom maker until both sides of it have been fully covered.

3 After the last loop, close the pom-pom maker and lock it.

4

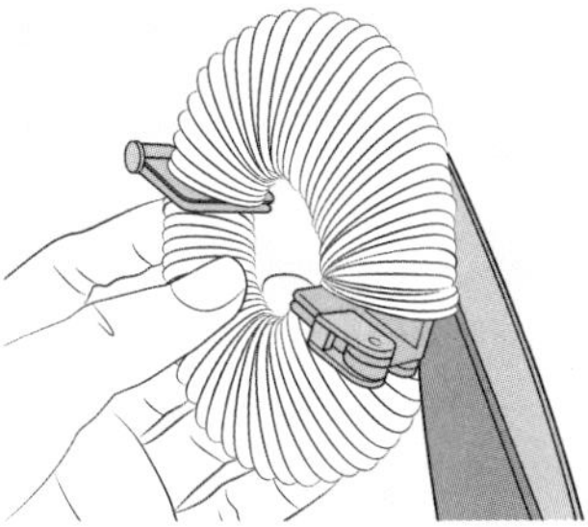

5

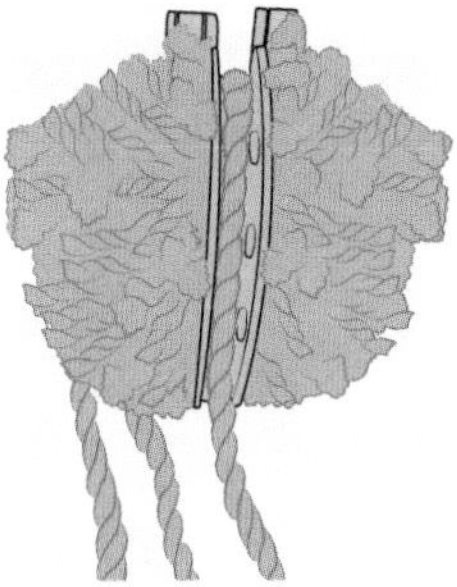

6

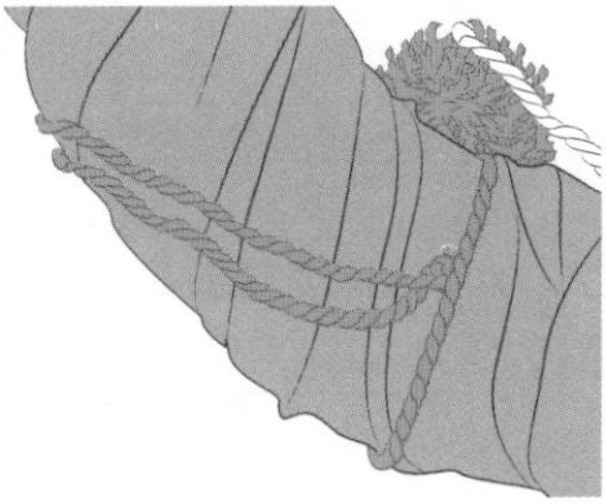

7

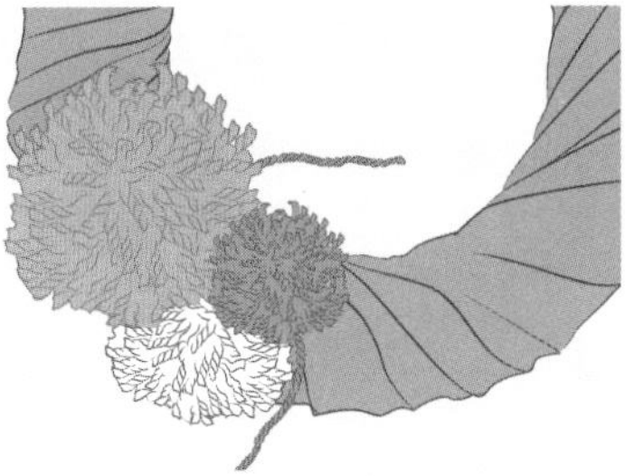

4 Using sharp, pointed scissors cut the yarn down the middle of the pom-pom maker and hold the yarn in place.

5 Wrap several strands of yarn and around the middle of the cut strands of the pom-pom, pull tight and knot securely. Leave two extra-long strands of yarn to tie around the wreath but trim any other strands to the length of the pom-pom.

6 Remove the pom-pom from the maker and, using the two long strands of yarn left, tie the pom-pom to the satin-covered wreath. Adjust until the pom-pom is securely attached and in the desired position on the wreath.

7 Using all the yarn colours and both sizes of pom-pom maker, create a total of 15 pom-poms. Arrange them on the wreath in your own design of unique colour and size combinations.

cushion cover

Tools and materials

- Rowan Big Wool super chunky (super bulky) yarn:
  - 1 x 100g (3½oz) ball in Vintage (085)
  - 1 x 100g (3½oz) ball in Prize (064)
  - 1 x 100g (3½oz) ball in White Hot (001)
- 12mm (US17) knitting needles
- Scissors
- Tapestry needle
- 3 buttons
- Cushion pad 50cm (19½in) square

Finished size:
54 X 50cm (21¼ x 19½in)

Tension:
9 sts x 10 rows = 10cm (4in) on 12mm (US17) needles

Technique used:
Stocking Stitch (see page 21)

Cushions are the finishing touch to any space: easy to add or take away and easy to move from one position to another in your home, they allow you to explore your immediate reaction to how they look on your chairs, sofa or bed. Made using extra-soft, chunky wool yarns in cream and muted tones, you will want to dive into the softness of these knitted cushions. Buttonhole and button fastenings also make them easy to remove.

i deserve a beautiful home where I feel happy

to make

1

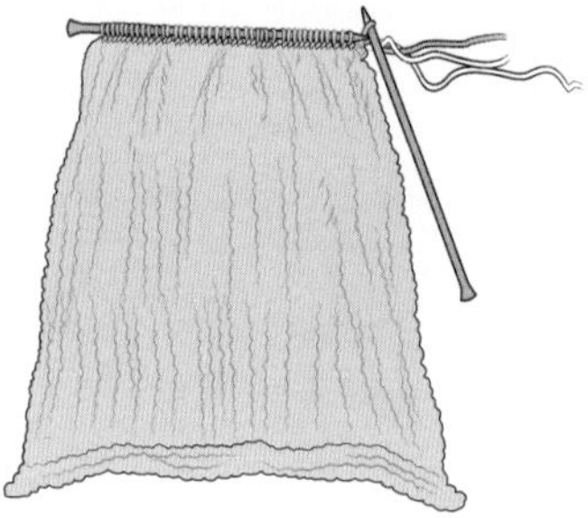

2

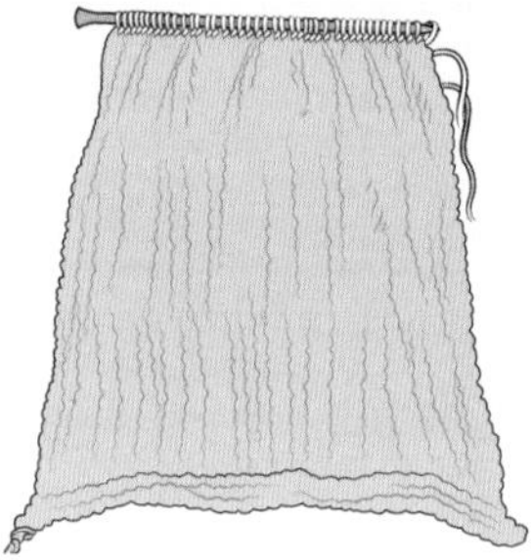

3

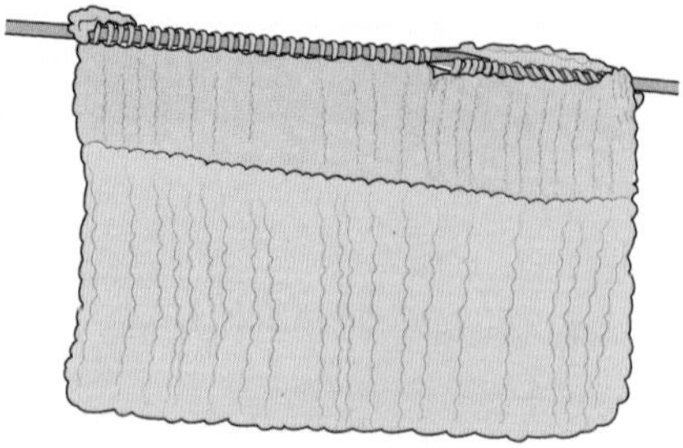

4

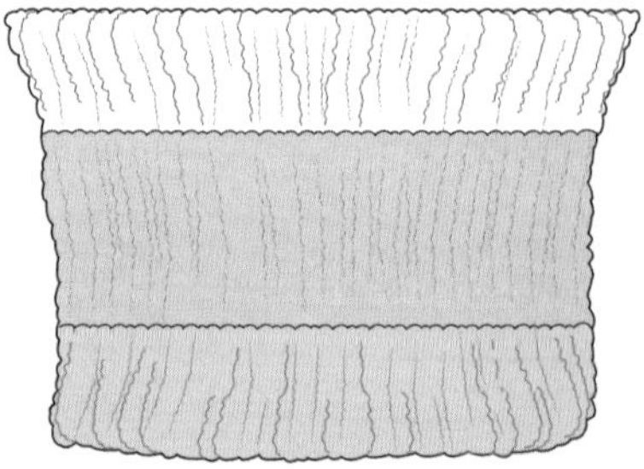

1 Cast on 42 stitches (see pages 13–15) in Vintage (purple) and knit 65 rows in stocking stitch (see page 21).

2 Change yarn colour (see page 32) to Prize (light pink) at end of row 65 (knit row).

3 Knit 18 rows with light pink. Change colour to White Hot (white) at end of row 18 (knit row).

4 Knit 19 rows in white.

5

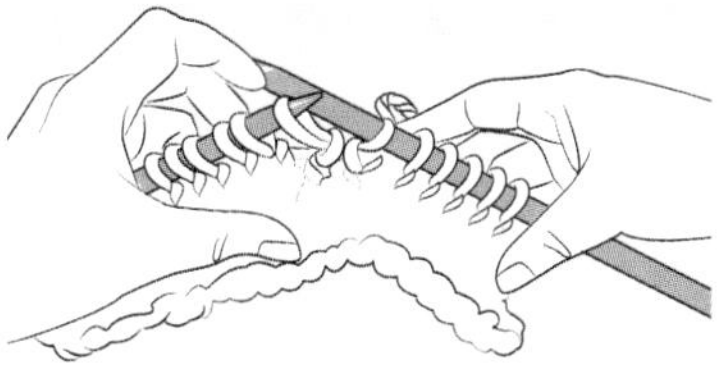

6

7

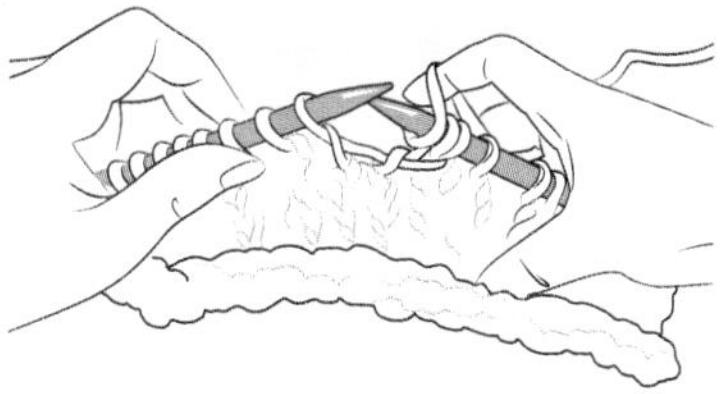

8

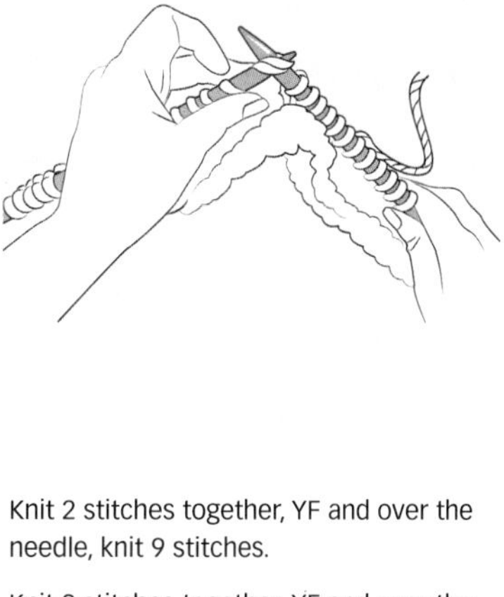

creating a row of buttonholes

5 Next row: (RS) Knit 8 stitches.

6 Knit 2 stitches together.

7 YF and over the needle (this will create a button hole), knit 9 stitches.

8 Knit 2 stitches together, YF and over the needle, knit 9 stitches.

9 Knit 2 stitches together, YF and over the needle, knit to end.

10 Next row: (WS) Purl to end.

11 Knit 3 rows. Cast off your knitting (see page 34) and weave in any loose ends using the tapestry needle (see page 40). You will have three buttonholes at the top of the cushion cover.

finishing

12 Lay down the knitted piece with the purl side facing upwards, the overall length should be approx 110cm (43¼in). Fold the knitted rectangle up by 100cm (39¾in).

13 Seam the sides of the cushion cover using mattress stitch (see page 36). This should be done on the knit side (outside of the cushion).

14 Sew on the buttons 6cm (2⅜in) from the top edge of the purple knit. Make sure they align with the buttonholes on the cast-off edge.

10

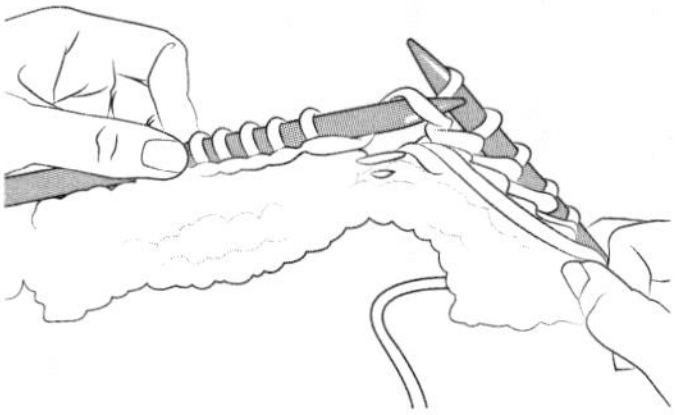

11

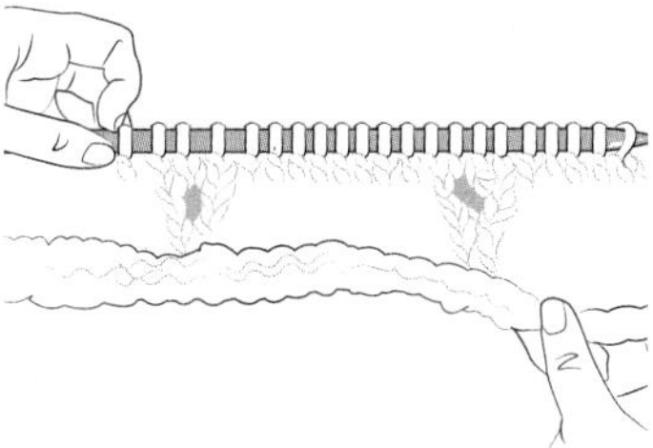

12

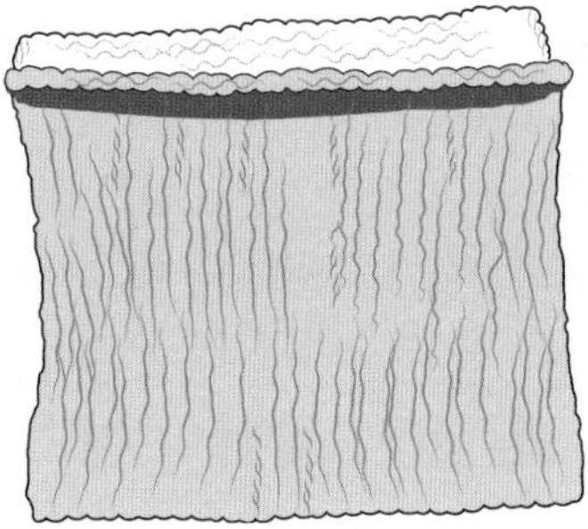

13

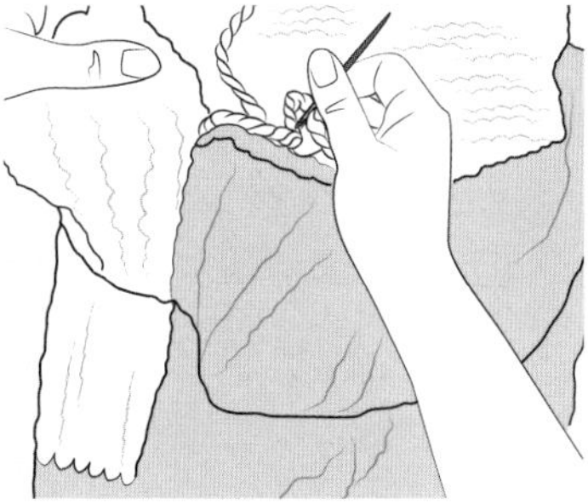

14

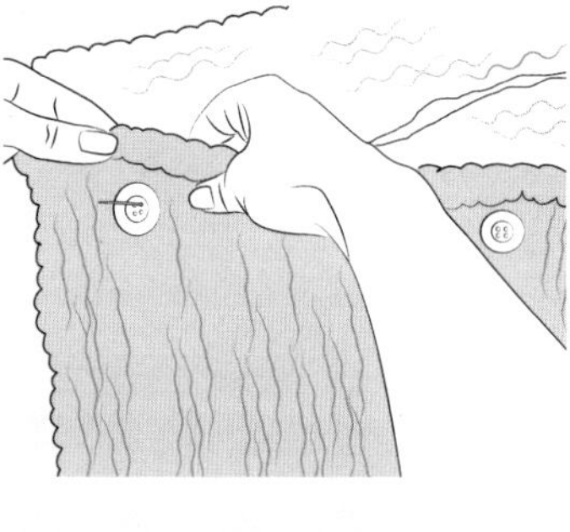

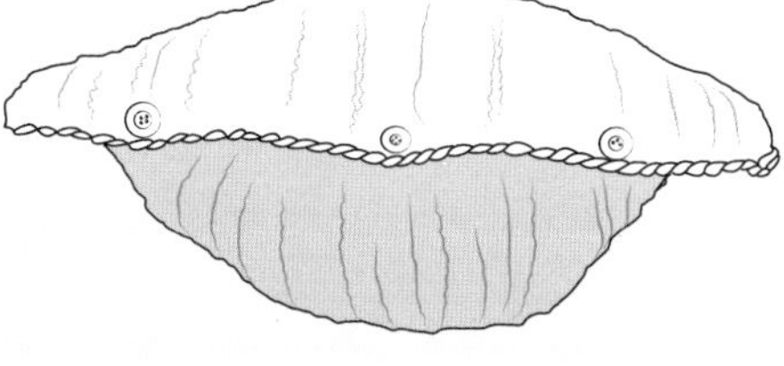

my confidence
is the best accessory!

Adding accessories can elevate your outfit and accentuate your style and combining textures and knitting techniques to create your own accessories to wear is especially exhilarating. In this chapter we'll be demonstrating stylish ways to create thick knitted scarfs, headbands, snoods, phone cases and even a handy bag to put all your essentials in. The designs in this chapter were inspired by the everyday person who wants their character to shine through in their unique makes. Details matter when it comes to accessorizing, so we've concentrated on using interesting yarns for the accessories, which you can combine with what you already have in your wardrobe. We hope you enjoy creating these projects and look forward to wearing your creations!

rib twist headband

Tools and materials

- 1 x 50g (1¾oz) ball of Debbie Bliss Paloma super chunky (super bulky) yarn in Burnt Orange (017)
- 8mm (US11) knitting needles
- Scissors
- Large tapestry needle

Finished circumference:
56cm (22in)

Tension:
12 sts x 18 rows =
10cm (4in) on 8mm
(US11) needles

Technique used:
1 x 1 Rib Stitch
(see page 30)

This stylish knitted headband is perfect for those days when you really want to keep your hair out of your face – useful and chic! It can also be worn as an ear warmer during the winter months, especially if you use thicker wools to make it

look good, feel good and give your problems a break

to make

1 Cast on 12 stitches (see pages 13–15).

2 Begin with 1 x 1 rib stitch (see page 30):
Row 1: *K1, p1, rep from * to end.
Knit 57 more rows in 1 x 1 rib stitch.

3 Cast off your knitting (see page 34) leaving a long yarn of at least 25cm (10in). You will need this for seaming at the end.

4 Fold cast-on and cast-off edges in half then hold an end in each hand with the fold at the bottom in the left hand and the fold at the top in the right hand.

5 Bring the ends together and insert the front layer of the right-hand end between the layers of the left-hand end, making a sandwich of alternating layers, left, right, left, right. Pin together.

6 Thread the long tail of the yarn using the large tapestry needle and begin to seam the four edges together – taking the yarn through each of the knitted loops on all the edges of the headband.

7 Turn the headband right side out so the seam is facing inwards. You now have a finished headband.

1

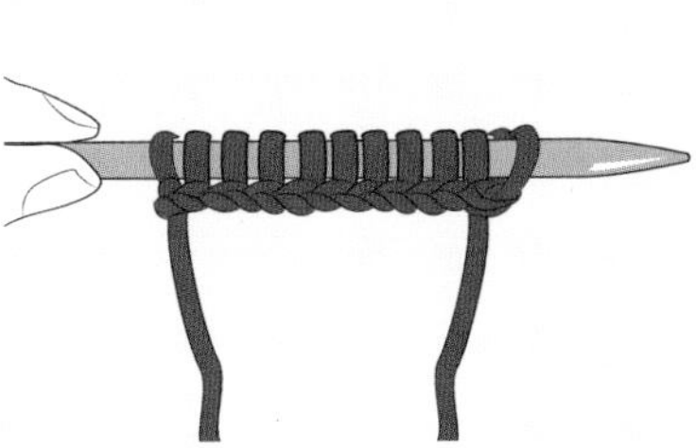

2

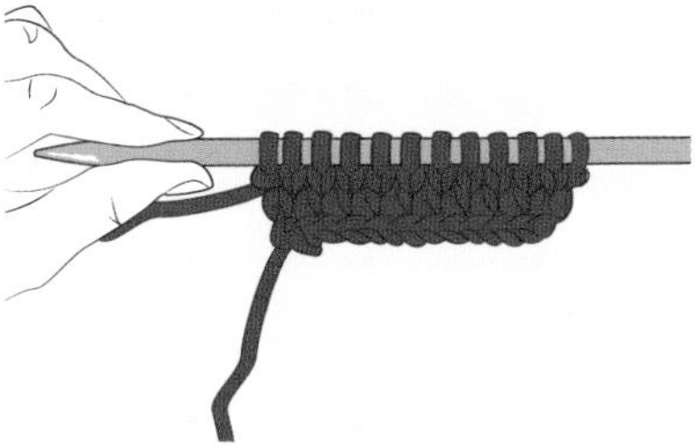

3

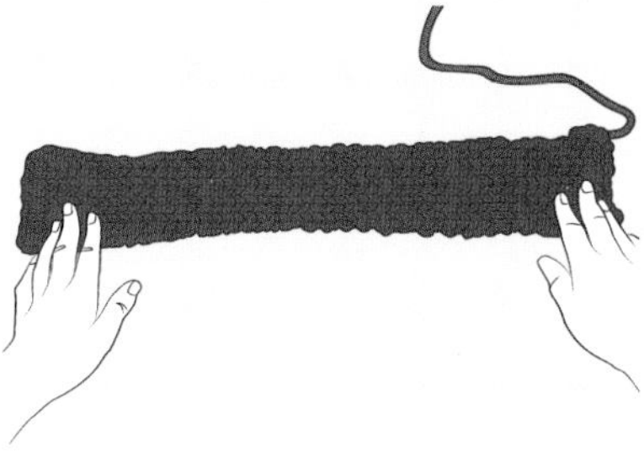

4

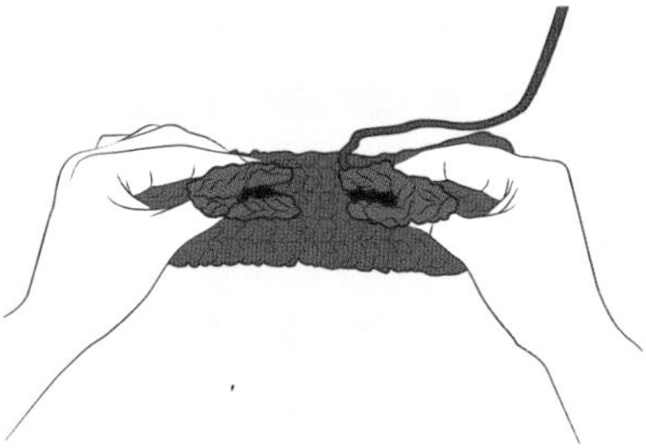

5

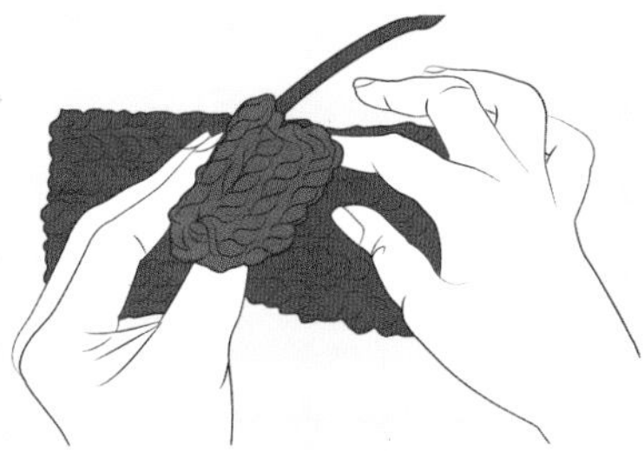

6

fingerless mittens

Tools and materials

- 1 x 100g (3½oz) ball of Cascade 220 Superwash Merino aran (worsted) yarn in Butterscotch (42)
- 5mm (US8) knitting needles
- Scissors
- Tapestry needle

Finished size:
approx 9cm (3½in) wide x 19cm (7½in) long

Tension:
18–20 sts = 10cm (4in) on 5mm (US8) needles

Techniques used:
1 x 1 Rib Stitch (see page 30), Stocking Stitch (see page 21)

Enjoy the feeling of the soft yarn used for these mittens while you make them and just think about the warmth they'll provide to your fingertips in the colder months! Keeping your fingers both toasty and fashionable, and unveiling them only when needed, is the main idea behind this design – these mittens are all about the user's comfort.

i believe in the vision, I trust the process

to make

1

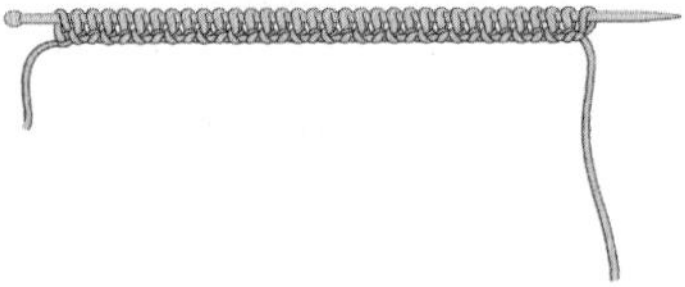

2

3

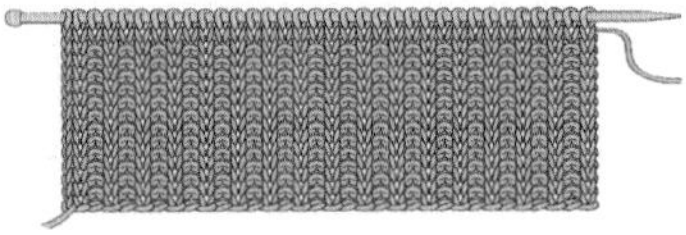

4

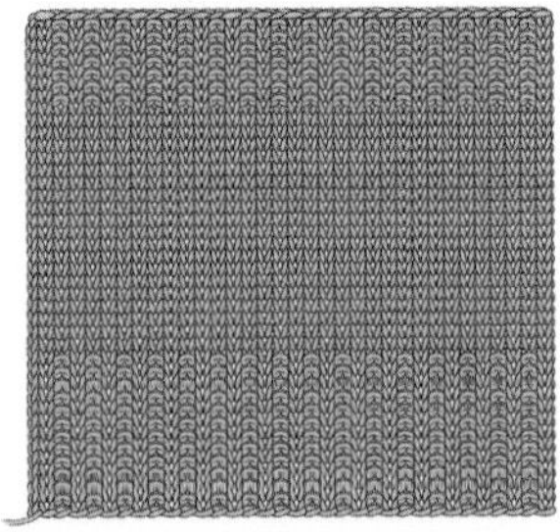

The rib cuff

1 Cast on 34 stitches (see pages 13–15) (it must be an even number). When casting on your stitches, leave a long cast-on tail of at least 15cm (6in). You will need this for seaming at the end of the pattern.

2 Begin with 1 x 1 rib stitch (see page 30):
Row 1: *K1, p1, rep from * to end.
Knit 13 more rows in 1 x 1 rib stitch until the cuff measures 7cm (2¾in).

stocking stitch hand section

3 Begin the stocking stitch section (see page 21):
Row 1: (RS) Knit.
Row 2: Purl.
Knit 20 more rows in stocking stitch until mitten measures 15cm (6in) from cast-on edge.

4 For the top of the mitten, continue in 1 x 1 rib stitch:
Row 1: *K1, p1, rep from * to end.
Knit 7 rows in 1 x 1 rib stitch until the mitten measures 19cm (7½in) from the cast-on edge.

5a

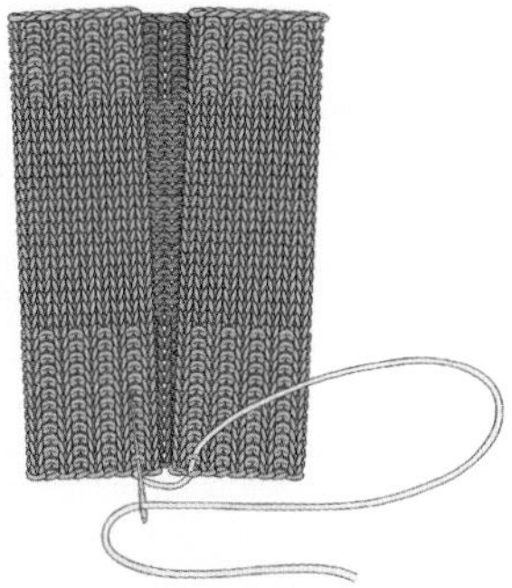

5b

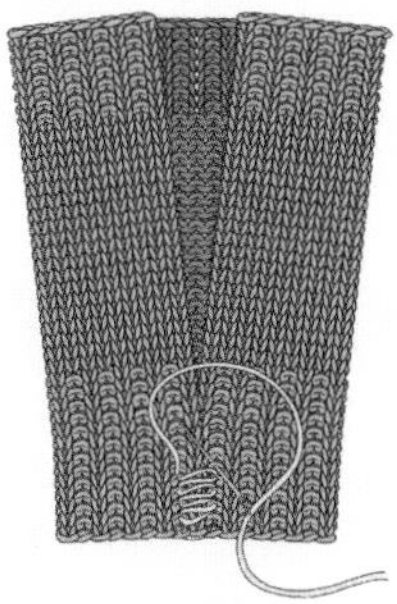

6

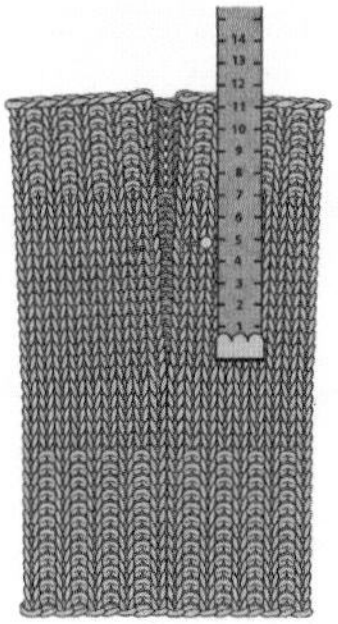

8

Repeat Row 1 for 7 rows until the mitten measures 19cm (7½in) from the cast-on edge.

joining the seams

5a Seam the two edges using mattress stitch (see page 36), using the long cast on tail, seam from the bottom upwards for 11cm (4¼in).

5b For this example we have seamed the edge using an alternative yarn colour.

6 Leave a gap of 5cm (2in) for the thumbhole.

7 Then, using a new length of yarn, begin seaming again until you reach the top of the mitten.

8 Fasten off and weave in any loose ends using the tapestry needle (see page 40).

striped mittens

Tools and materials

- Cascade 220 Superwash Merino aran (worsted) yarn:
  - 1 x 100g (3½oz) ball in Butterscotch (42)
  - 1 x 100g (3½oz) ball in Ecru (36)
- 5mm (US8) knitting needles
- Scissors
- Tapestry needle

Finished size:
8cm (3in) wide x 19cm (7in) long

Tension:
18–20 sts = 10cm (4in) on 5mm (US8) needles

Techniques used:
Stocking Stitch
(see page 21)

Why not create a contrast and use two colours to create your winter mittens? Select shades that work well together to produce a feel-good accessory that will add personality to any outfit. You could also try using even more colours!

good things are happening

to make

1 Cast on 29 stitches (see pages 13–15) in Butterscotch (yellow) yarn. Leave a long cast-on tail of at least 15cm (6in). You will need this for seaming at the end.

2 Knit 20 rows in stocking stitch (see page 21).

3 Change yarn colour to Ecru (cream) (see page 32)

3a knit 20 more rows in stocking stitch. Cast off your knitting (see page 34) and weave in any loose ends (except the cast-on tail) using the tapestry needle (see page 40).

4 Blocking: If you have used merino wool for your mittens, you can soak them in lukewarm water for 15 minutes, then leave them to air dry and block them using pins on a flat surface (see page 42).

5 Use mattress stitch (see page 36) and the long cast-on tail you left at the beginning to seam the two edges of both mittens. Work from the bottom upwards for 11cm (4³/8in).

6 Leave a gap of 5cm (2in) for the thumbhole and, using a new length of yarn, begin seaming again until you reach the top of the mittens.

7 Cast on and weave in any loose ends using the tapestry needle.

1

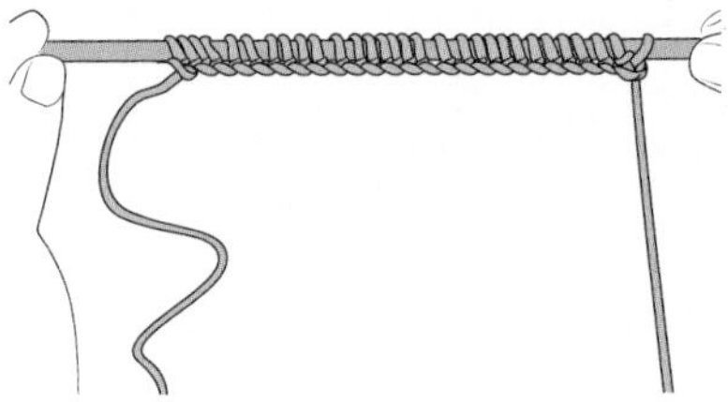

3a

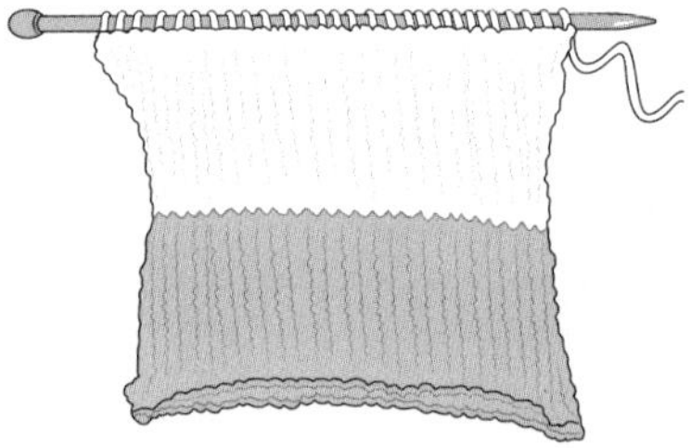

6

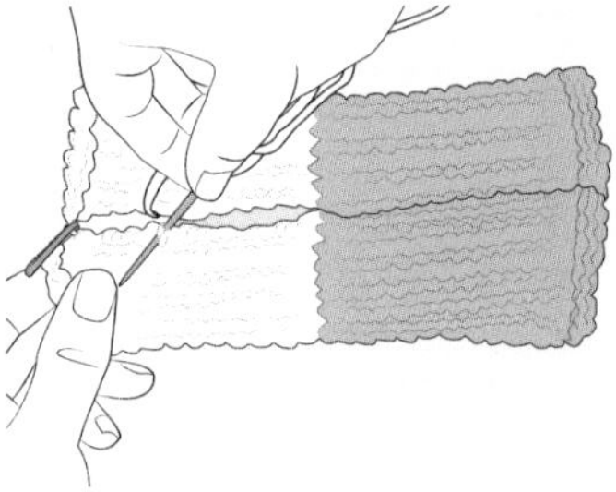

2

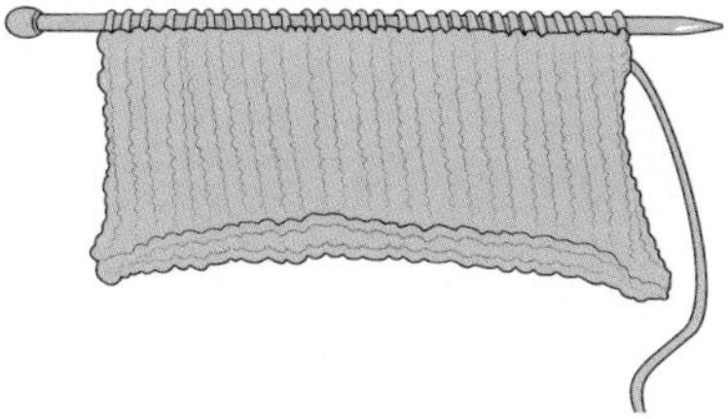

3

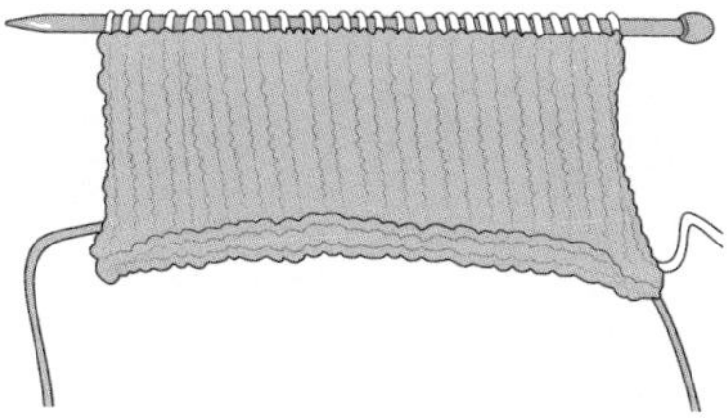

4

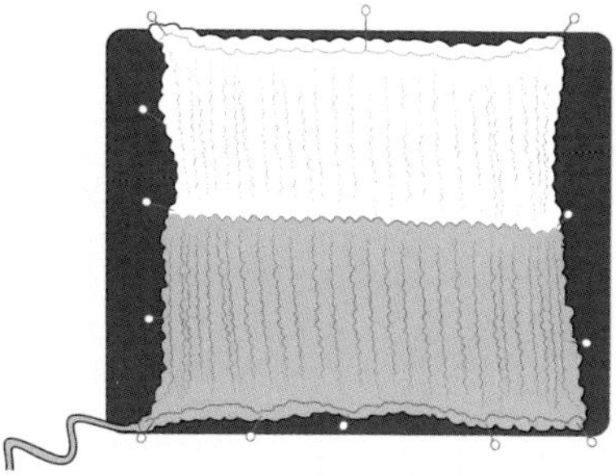

5

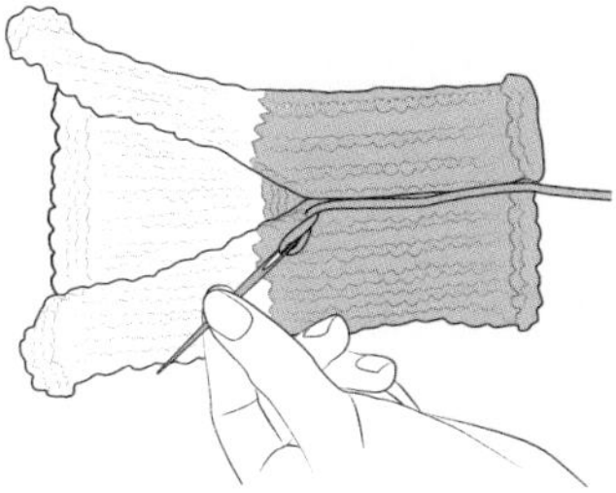

7

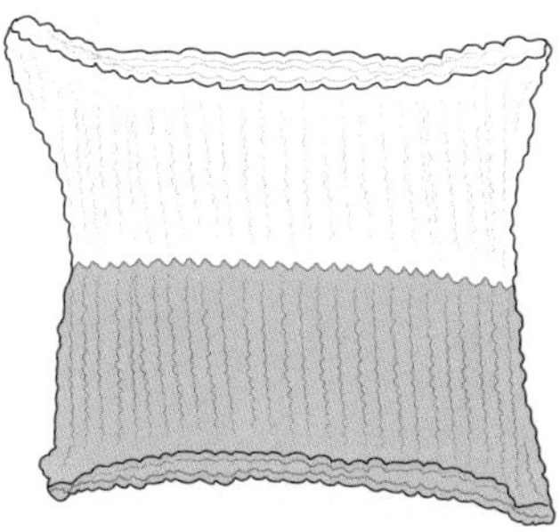

fringed scarf

Tools and materials

- 2 x 250g (8¾ oz) balls of Cascade Magnum Tweed super chunky (super bulky) yarn in Olive Oil (09)
- 12mm (US17) knitting needles
- Scissors
- Tapestry needle
- Tape measure or ruler
- Crochet hook

Finished length:
162cm (63¾in)

Tension:
6–8 sts = 10cm (4in) on 12mm (US) needles

Technique used:
Garter Stitch
(see page 20)

Relax into the gentle rhythm of every stitch as you knit this garter stitch scarf. Working in the same stitch row after row is a calming and therapeutic experience. This simple, elegant design is finished off with a flourish by adding soft fringing to each end. Whatever the weather, this thick, soft, hand-stitched scarf is guaranteed to provide warmth, joy and comfort whenever you wear it.

self-confidence is what I thrive on.
nothing is impossible, and life is great

to make

1

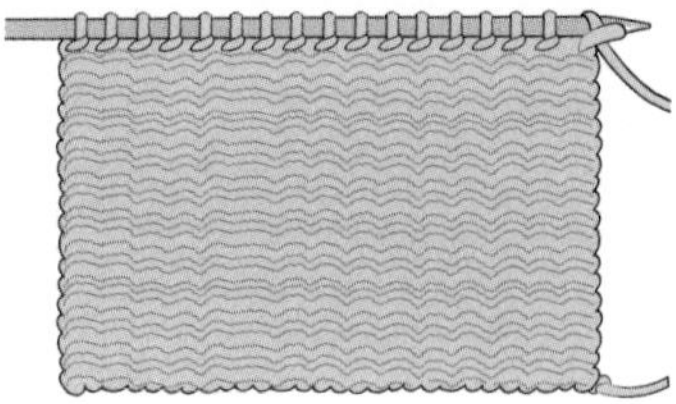

3

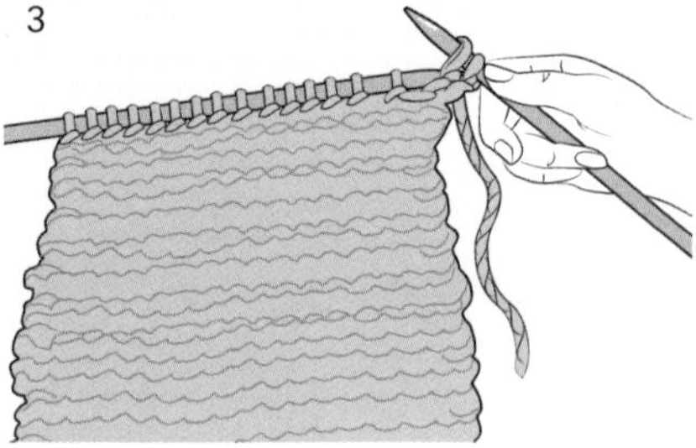

attaching fringing

1

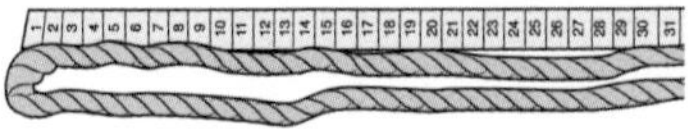

2

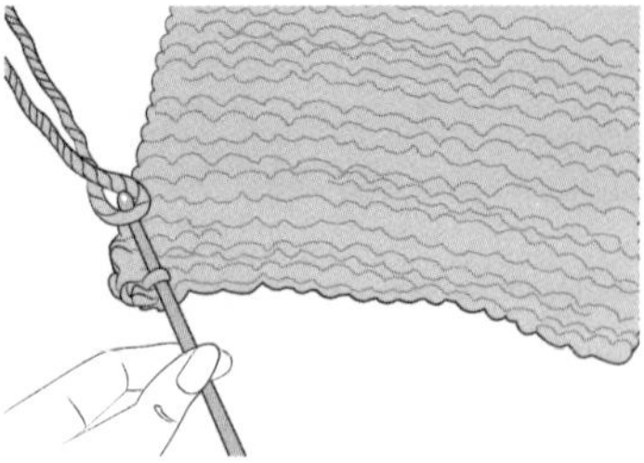

1 Cast on 17 stitches (see pages 13–15) and knit 182 rows of garter stitch (see page 20).

2 Begin to cast off your knitting (see page 34). Knit 2 stitches and take the first stitch over the second stitch.

3 Knit the next stitch and continue to cast off until you reach the last stitch Cut your yarn leaving a 10cm (4in) tail and take the tail of the yarn through the loop to fasten off.

attaching fringing

1 Measure 60 cm (23½in) of yarn – or the required length for fringing – and cut the length of yarn.

2 Insert the crochet hook into your selected stitch on the cast-on edge of the scarf. Place the folded loop of fringing onto the crochet hook.

3

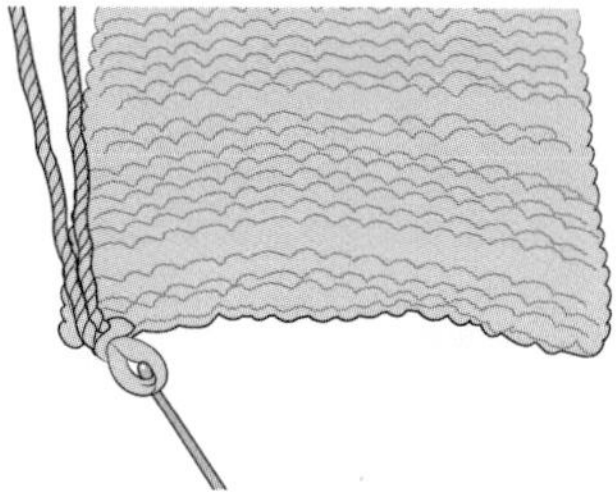

4

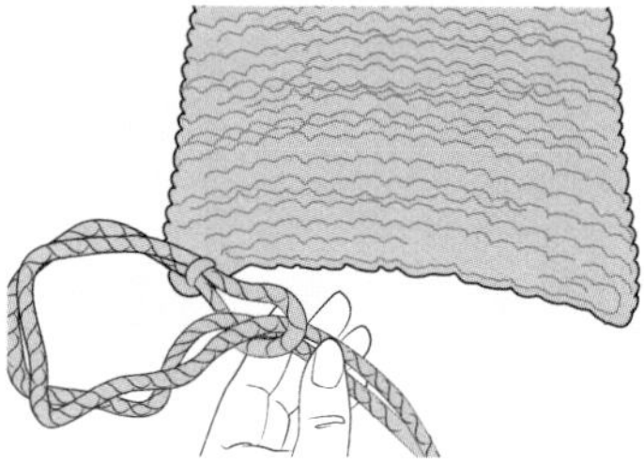

5

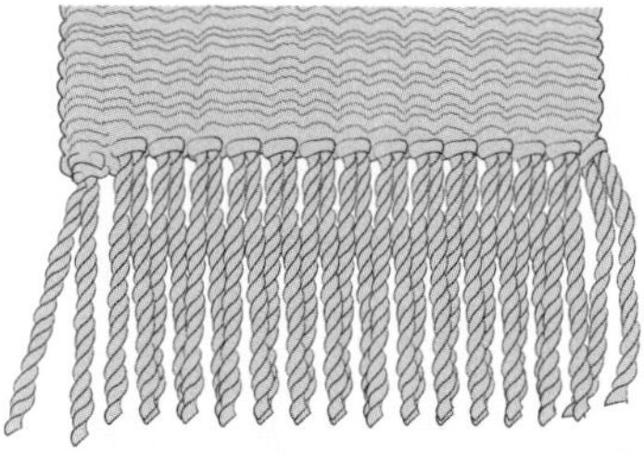

6

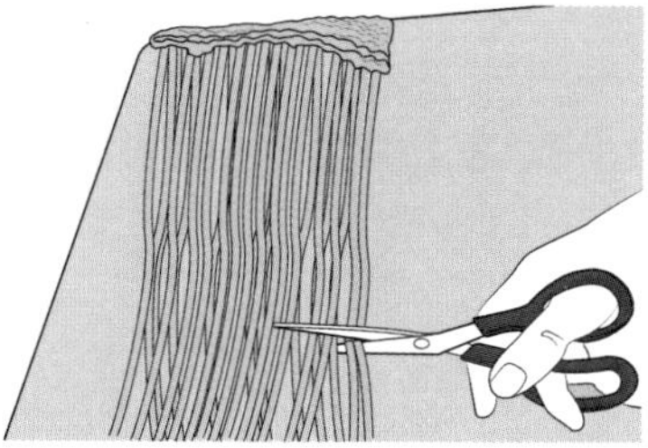

3 Pull the loop of fringing through the knitted stitch to the front.

4 Now hook the tails of your yarn with the crochet hook and pull them through the loop of the yarn. Pull on the tails to tighten the knot.

5 Repeat the same process along the length of the edge of the scarf. When you have attached the fringing to one side of your scarf, repeat the fringing process on the other side.

6 When all fringing has been attached to the scarf, lay your work flat and trim the fringing to the same length on both ends.

moss stitch snood

Tools and materials

- 1 x 250g (8¾oz) ball of Cascade Magnum Tweed super chunky (super bulky) yarn in Camel (08)
- 12mm (US17) knitting needles
- Scissors
- Tapestry needle

Finished circumference:
91cm (38¾in)

Tension:
6–8 sts = 10cm (4in) on 12mm (US17) needles

Technique used:
Moss Stitch
(see page 22)

An exciting item for your wardrobe, especially as you catch a glimpse of yourself in the mirror before you head out. The snood is a statement piece that can quickly turn into a favourite piece to wear again and again. You can explore different knit techniques to create the snood and experiment with different yarn textures using this simple moss stitch technique.

i fill my mind with positive and nourishing thoughts

to make

1

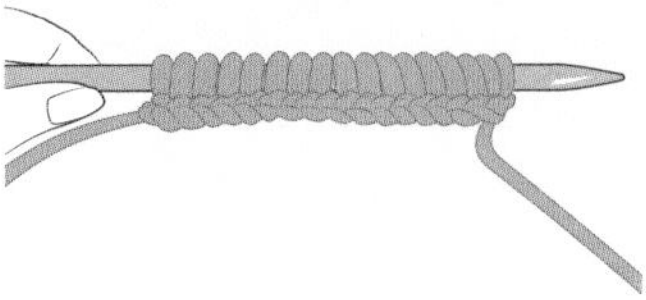

1a

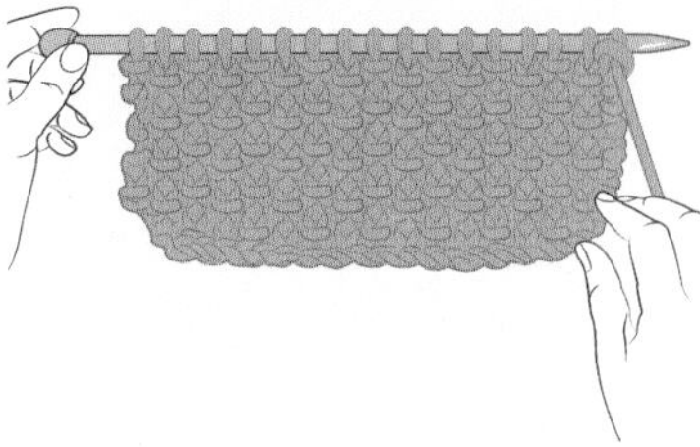

2

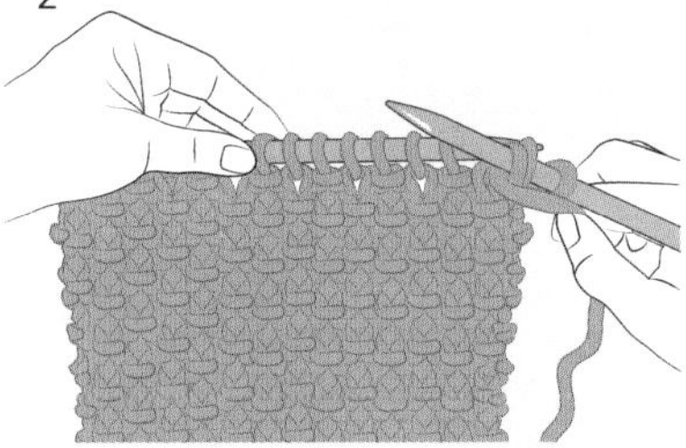

3

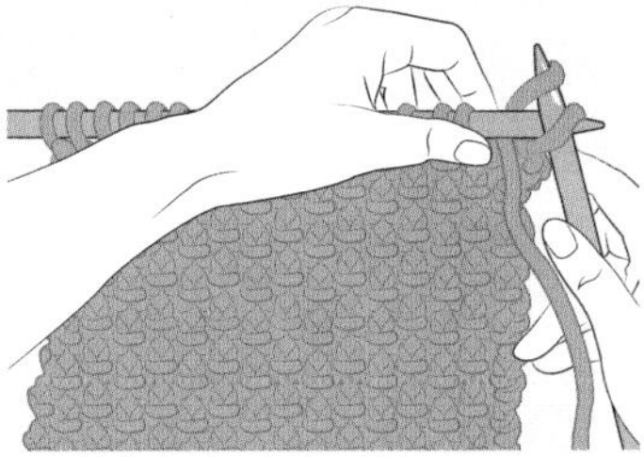

1 Cast on 17 stitches.

1a Knit 90 rows in moss stitch (see page 22).

2 Now cast off, continuing with the knit and purl moss stitch pattern. Knit the first stitch onto your RH needle and then purl the next stitch.

3 Take the first stitch over the second stitch. Knit the next stitch and take the first stitch over the second stitch. Purl the next stitch and continue to cast off until you reach the last stitch on the needle. Cut your yarn leaving a long yarn tail for seaming and take the tail of the yarn through the loop to fasten off. Weave in any loose ends using the tapestry needle (see page 40).

4

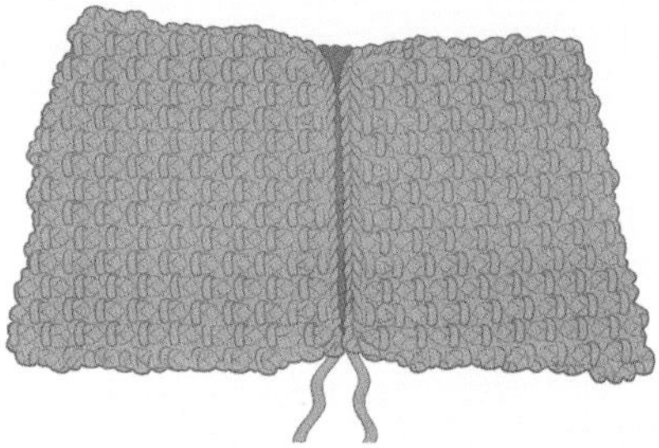

5

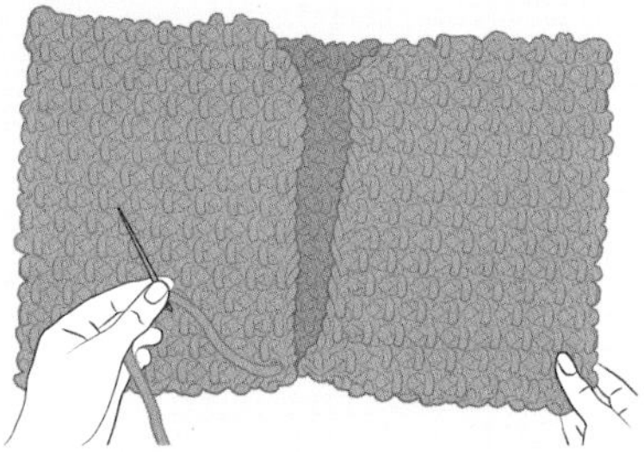

6

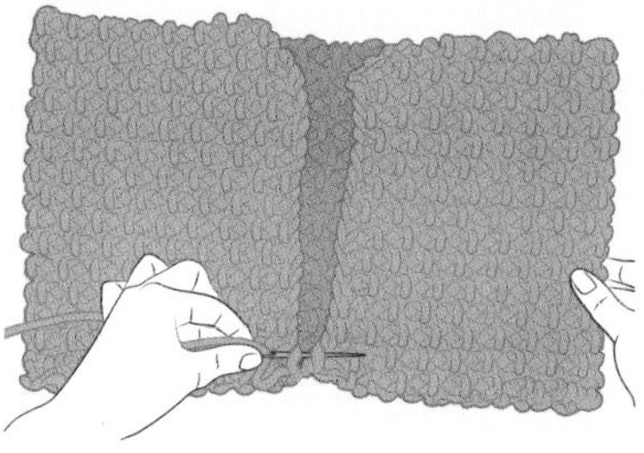

7

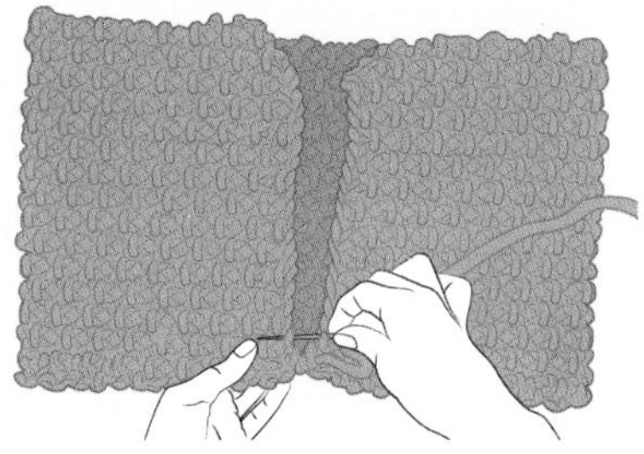

4 Bring the cast-on and cast-off edges together, aligned so they are in the centre of your knit.

5 Use a flat seam (see page 38) to join the edges of the snood. Thread the tapestry needle with the long tail of yarn from the cast-off edge and bring it through the loop on the bottom left of your cast-on edge.

6 Now take the yarn from the left to the corresponding edge stitch on the right to begin joining the edges and creating a seam.

7 Continue stitching, taking the needle from right to left, then left to right until you have stitched the length of the join.

striped snood

Tools and materials

- Cascade Magnum Tweed super chunky (super bulky yarn:
  - 1 x 250g (8¾oz) ball in Camel (08)
  - 1 x 250g (8¾oz) ball in Smoke Blue (02)
- 12mm (US17) knitting needles
- Scissors
- Tapestry needle

Finished size:
102cm (40in)

Tension:
6–8 sts = 10cm (4in) on 12mm (US17) needles

Technique used:
Moss Stitch
(see page 22)

The knitted snood is the perfect beginner friendly knit project, using your favourite chunky wool yarn. The moss stitch snood is guaranteed to give you constant warmth, joy and comfort during a cold or mild autumnal day. A must have winter accessory, experiment with different hues of brown, green or blue yarns. Perfect for those autumn forest walks.

happiness is a choice. i base my happiness on my own accomplishments and the blessings I've been given

to make

1 Cast on 17 stitches (see pages 13–15) using Camel (beige).

2 Knit for 20 rows in moss stitch (see page 22).

3a Change colour to Smoke Blue (blue) (see page 32).

3b Knit 20 rows in moss stitch. You will now have the first colour block change in blue.

4 Change colour to beige and knit 20 rows in moss stitch.

5 Change colour to blue and knit 20 rows in moss stitch.

1

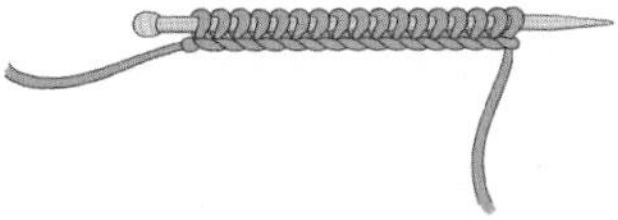

2

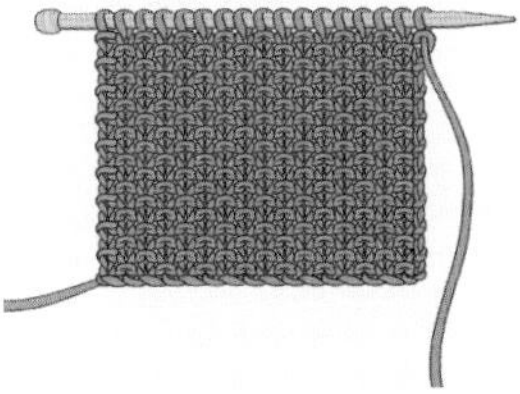

3a

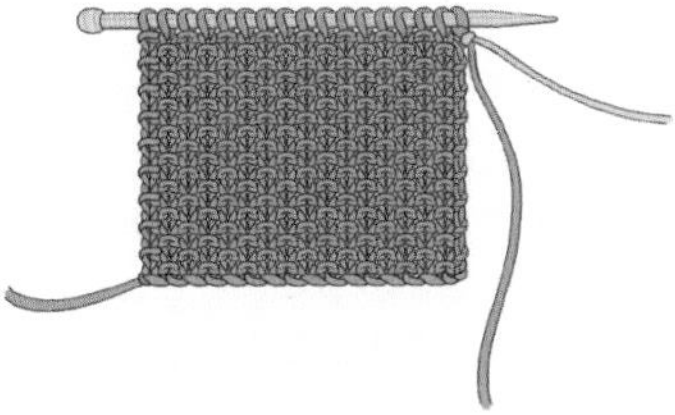

3b

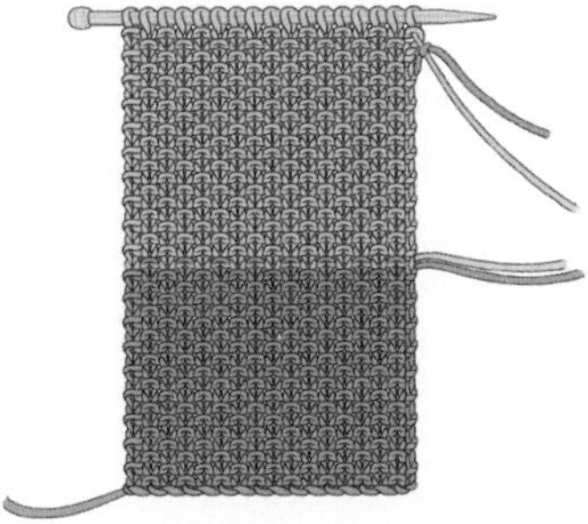

4

5

6 Change colour to beige and knit 12 rows in moss stitch.

7a Cast off your knitting (see page 34) leaving a long tail end for seaming.

7b Weave in any loose ends using the tapestry needle (see page 40).

8 Bring the cast-on and cast-off edges together, aligned so they are in the centre of your knit.

9 Use a flat seam (see page 38) to join the edges of the snood. Thread the tapestry needle with the long tail of yarn and bring it through the loop on the bottom left of your cast-off edge.

10 Now take the yarn from the left to the corresponding edge stitch on the right to begin joining the edges and creating a seam. Continue stitching, taking the needle from right to left, then left to right until you have stitched the length of the join.

6

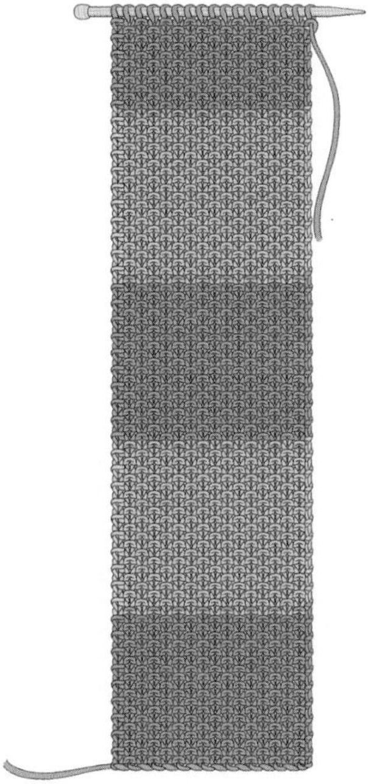

7a

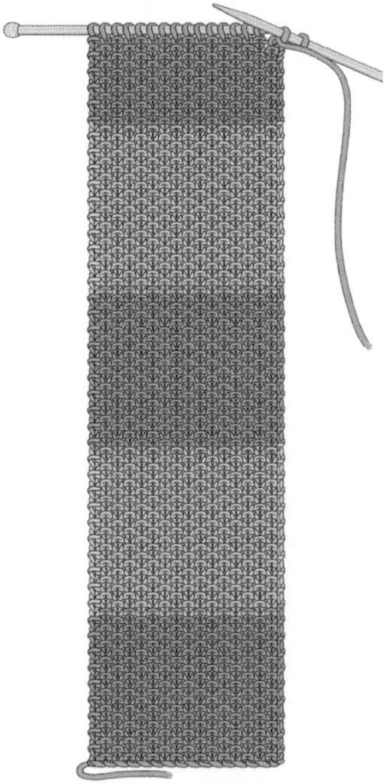

7b

8

9

10

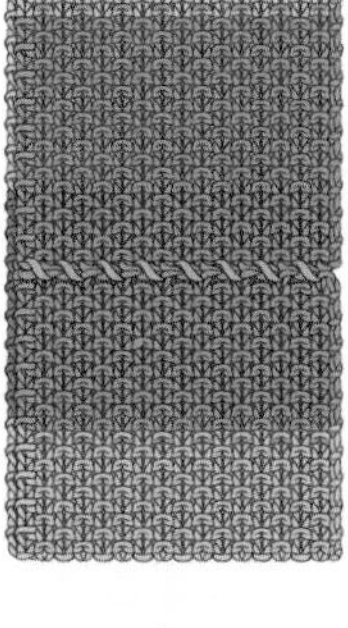

basketweave bag

Tools and materials

- 1 x 500g Hoooked Spesso Chunky (bulky) yarn in Spring
- 10mm (US15) knitting needles
- 6mm (USJ/10) crochet hook
- 2 x hook bag clasps
- Tapestry needle
- Button or bead
- Scissors
- Tape measure or ruler

Finished size:
16 x 29 x 3cm
(16¼ x 11½ x 1¼in)

Tension:
14 sts x 12 rows
= 10cm (4in) on 10mm (US15) needles

Technique used:
Basketweave Stitch
(see page 24)

This handy little bag is just right for carrying around all your essentials. Use brightly coloured yarn to make an impact – and turn this simple bag into a statement piece. You could also knit one row using another vibrant colour to make a strap, then attach the strap and you have created a cross-body bag!

i seek progress over perfection, and community over competition

to make

1 Cast on a total of 24 stitches (a multiple of 8 stitches) (see pages 13–15).

2 Begin the basketweave stitch pattern (see page 24) :
Row 1: *K4, p4, rep from * to end.
Rows 2 to 4: Repeat row 1.

3 Row 5: *P4, k4, rep from * to end
Rows 6 to 8: Repeat row 5.

4 Repeat steps 2 and 3 four more times.

5 Repeat step 2 once more.

6 Cast off your knitting (see page 34) and weave in any loose ends using the tapestry needle (see page 40).

7 Decide which side of your knit will be on the outside of the bag and place the knit down with the right side up. Fold up the bottom of the piece by 14cm (5½in) to create the inside pocket of the clutch bag.

8 Thread your tapestry needle with yarn and seam the edges using mattress stitch (see page 36), stitching through the corresponding bars on the end stitches of either side.

9 Now that you have seamed both sides, turn the pouch right side out.

10 Stitch a bead or button of your choice halfway across the top flap of the bag.

2

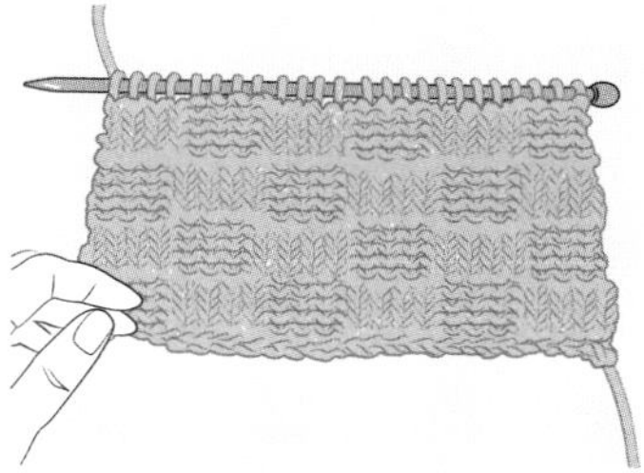

4

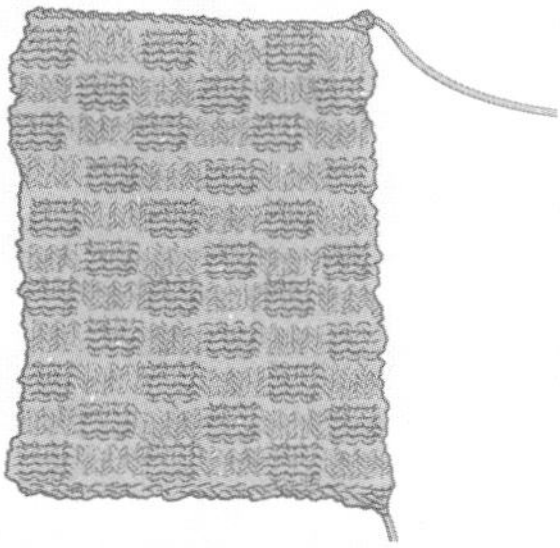

7

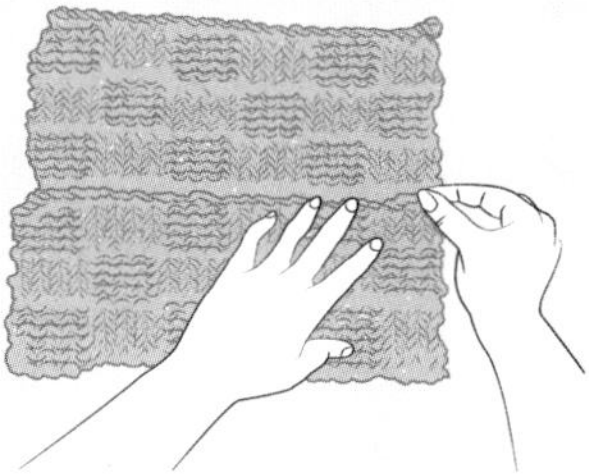

8

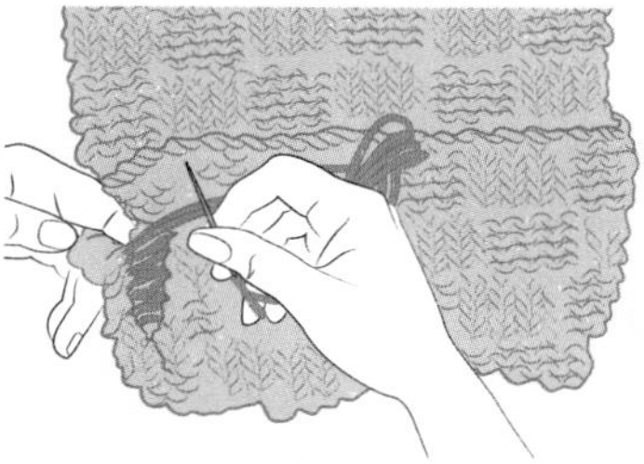

9

10

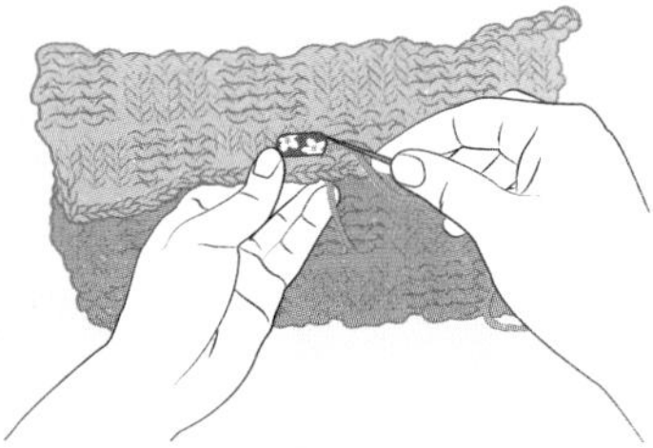

creating your bag straps

1 Using the crochet hook, create a slip knot on your hook.

2 Holding the hook with the slipknot in your right hand, use your left hand to wrap the working yarn over the crochet hook from back to front.

3 Pull the hook down, catching the yarn and pull the yarn through the slip knot. You have just created one crochet chain stitch.

4 Wrap the working yarn around the over the hook from back to front. Pull the hook down, catching the yarn and pull the yarn through the loop. Repeat step 4 until your length of chain measures 104cm (41in).

5 Now attach your bag clasps to the corners on either side of your bag. Take your chain-stitch cord and place the end of the yarn through the loop of the bag clasps.

6 Using the crochet hook or your fingers create a knot to attach the cord to the bag clasp.

7 Weave in any loose ends on the strap and repeat Steps 14 and 15 on the other corner of the bag to secure your straps.

1

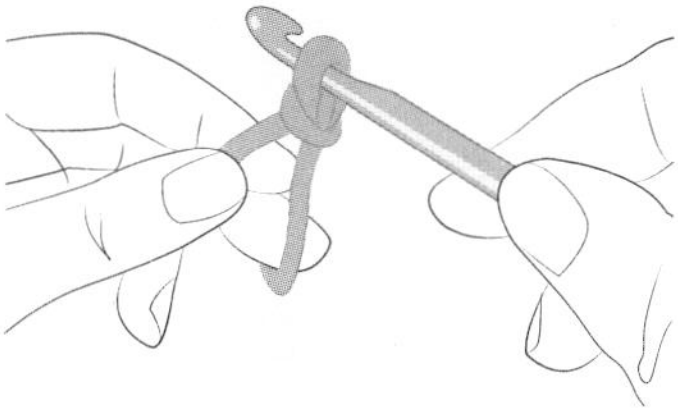

2

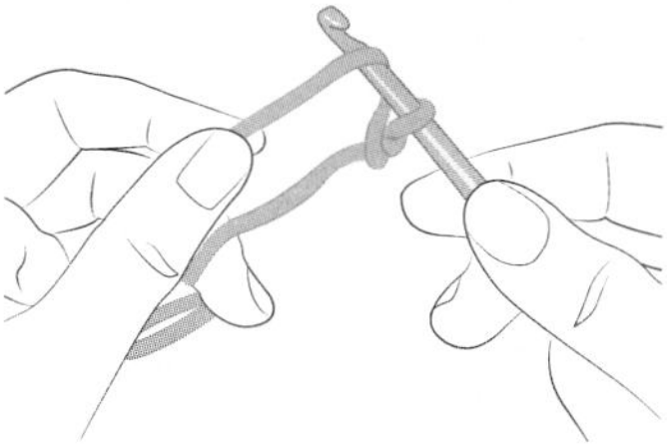

3

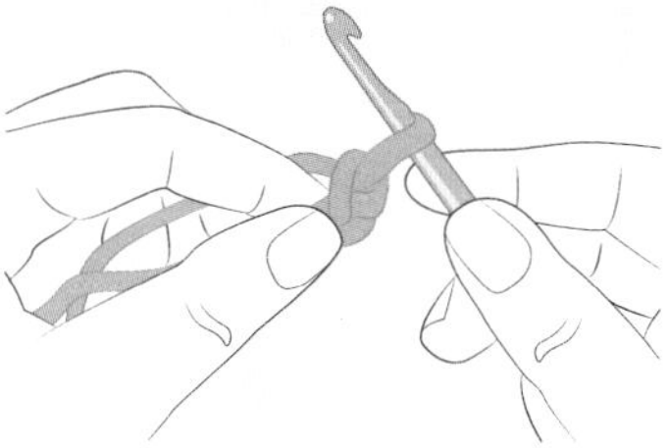

4

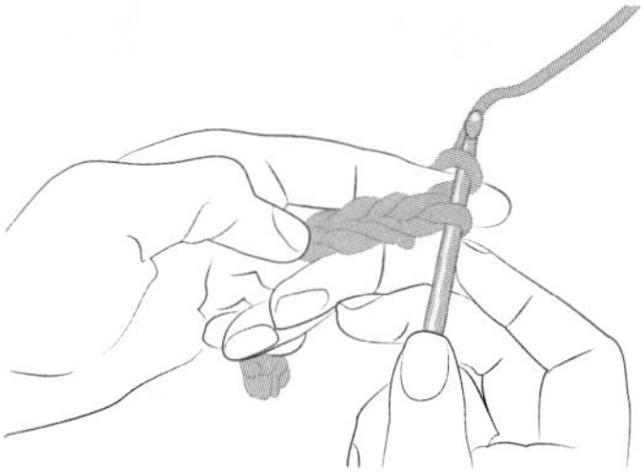

5

6

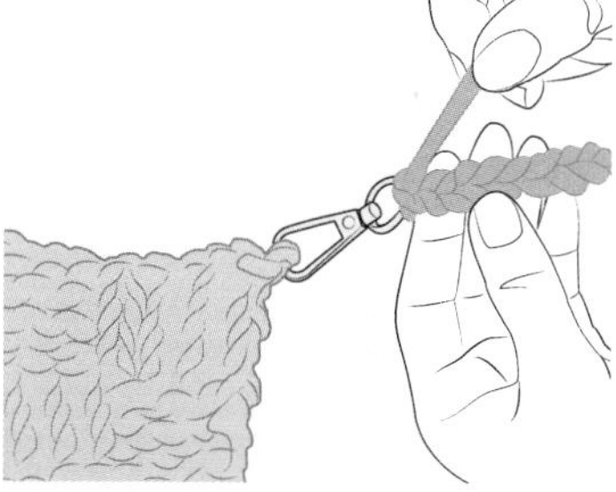

small basketweave bag

Tools and materials

- 1 x 250g (8¾oz) ball of Paintbox Recycled Big Cotton super chunky (super bulky) yarn in Orange (013)
- 10mm (US15) knitting needles
- 6mm (USJ/10) crochet hook
- Tapestry needle

Finished size:
13 x 18 x 3cm
(5¼ x 7 x 1¼in)

Tension:
9 stitches and 11 rows = 10cm (4in) on 10mm (US15) needles

Technique used:
Basketweave Stitch
(see page 24)

Creating something with your own hands is deeply enjoyable and satisfying. Allow your creativity to flourish, take time to enjoy the process of combining techniques and, if you wish, experimenting with colour and texture. This knitted bag is portable and extremely handy for carrying everything you need when you're on-the-go.

time is the most valuable resource;
therefore, I spend it wisely

to make

1 Cast on a total of 16 stitches (a multiple of 8 stitches).

2 Begin with the basketweave stitch pattern:
Row 1: *K4, p4, rep from * to end.
Rows 2 to 4: Repeat row 1.
Row 5: *P4, k4, rep from * to end.
Rows 6 to 8: Repeat row 5.

3 Repeat step 2 three times more until you have knit 32 rows. Cast off your knitting (see page 34) and weave in any loose ends using the tapestry needle (see page 40).

4 Decide which side of your basket stitch pattern will be on the outside of the bag and face this towards the outside. Fold the knitted piece in half to create the inside pocket of the bag. Thread your tapestry needle with yarn and seam the edges using mattress stitch (see page 36), stitching through the corresponding bars on the end stitches of either side.

2

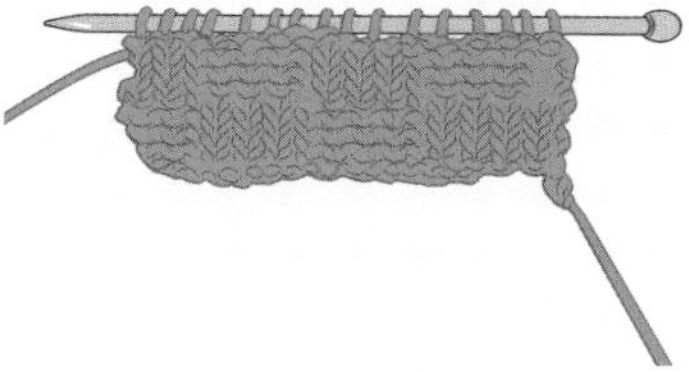

3

4

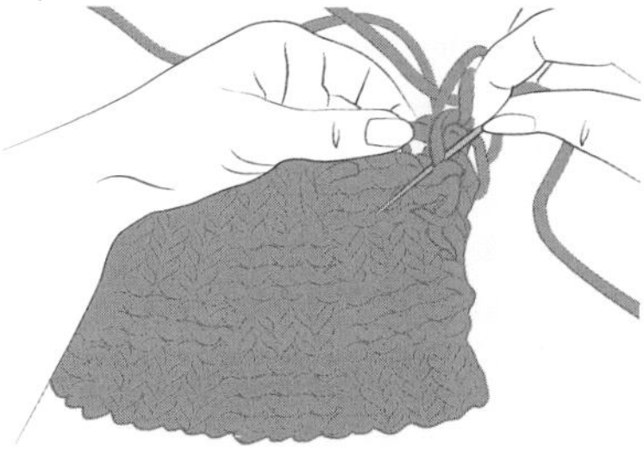

bag strap

1. Cast on 4 stitches.
2. Knit for 52 rows in garter stitch (see page 20) until the strap measures 51cm (20in). Cast off your knitting (see page 34) and weave in any loose ends using the tapestry needle (see page 40).
3. Secure one end of the bag strap to the inside seam of the bag using a pin.
4. Thread your tapestry needle and stitch the bag strap along the inside seam of the bag by looping the yarn through the stitches.
5. Also secure the bag strap on the outside of the seam by going through the knitted loops with your yarn and tapestry needle.
6. Repeat steps 3–5 on the other side of the bag to secure the strap.

1

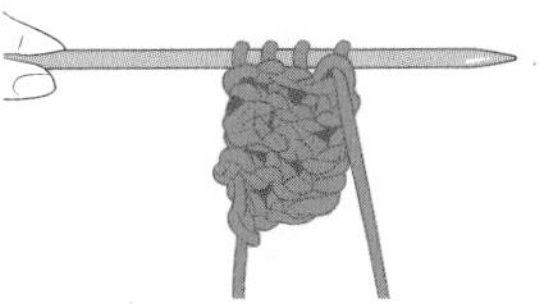

2

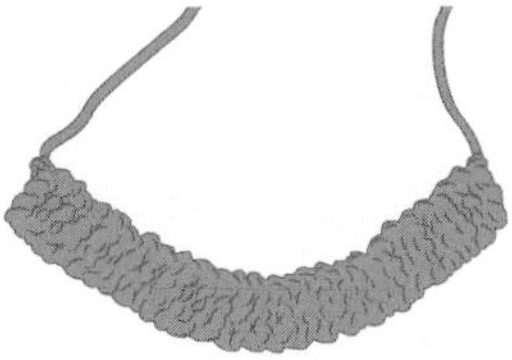

3

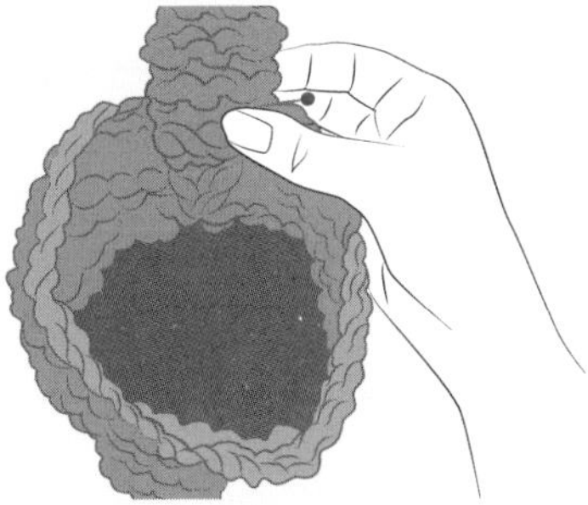

4

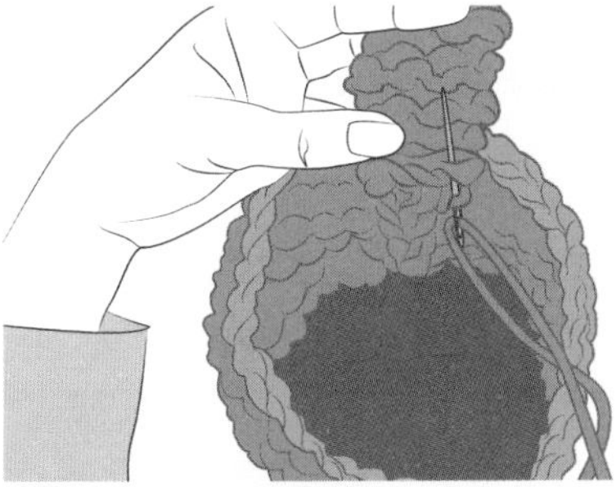

5

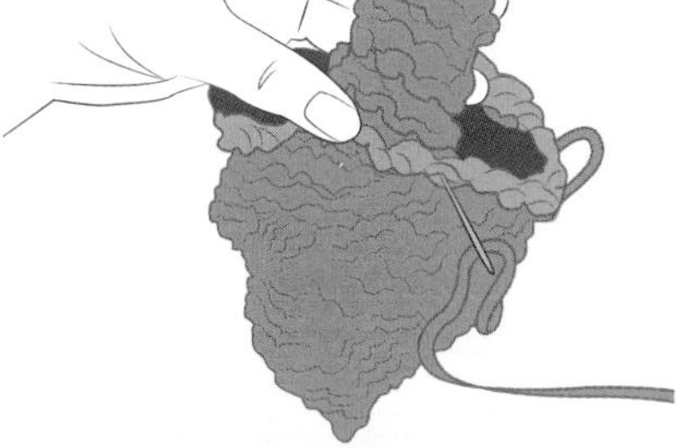

6

phone case

Making knitted accessories for essential everyday items like your mobile phone helps enable you to learn what is important in your everyday life. It's also one way to improve the details of your life little by little, stitch by stitch – let it inspire you to learn ways of boosting your creativity, right down to the finer details.

Tools and materials

- Rowan Softyak DK (light worsted) yarn in:
  - 1 x 50g (1¾oz) ball in Pampas (235)
  - 1 x 50g (1¾oz) ball in Jaune (252)
- 1 button
- 5mm (US8) knitting needles
- Tapestry needle
- Scissors
- Sewing needle
- Sewing thread in a matching colour

Finished size:
7 x 15 cm (2¾ x 6in)

Tension:
22 sts x 30 rows
= 10cm (4in) on 5mm
(US8) knitting needles

Technique used:
2 x 2 Rib Stitch
(see page 31)

to make

1 Cast on 20 stitches (see pages 13–15) with the two yarn colours together.

2 Knit 27 rows in 2 x 2 rib (see page 31).

3 Cast off your knitting (see page 34) and weave in any loose ends using the tapestry needle (see page 40).

4a Fold the phone case in half and use mattress stitch (see page 36) to sew the bottom edges together.

4b Use mattress stitch to sew the side seam together.

5 Continue to sew the side seams together, along the side of the phone case.

6 Position the button at the top of the phone case, directly under the cast-off edge. Sew the button onto the case using a sewing needle and matching thread.

i think outside of the box and colour outside of the lines

1

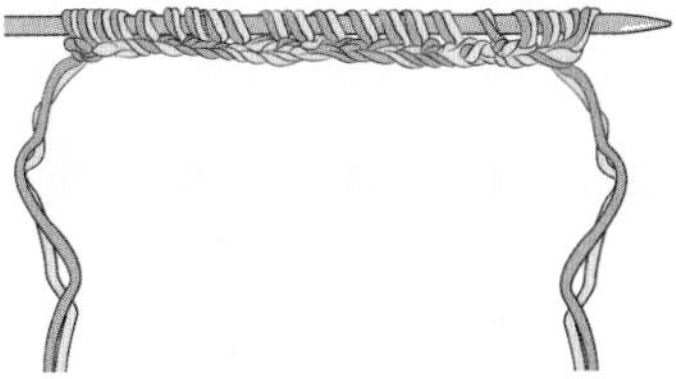

2

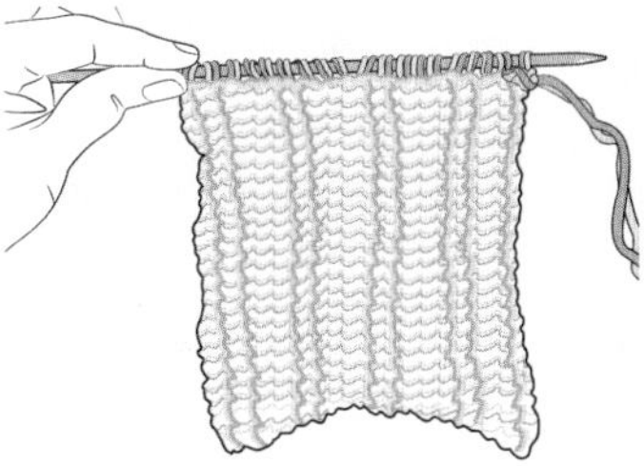

4a

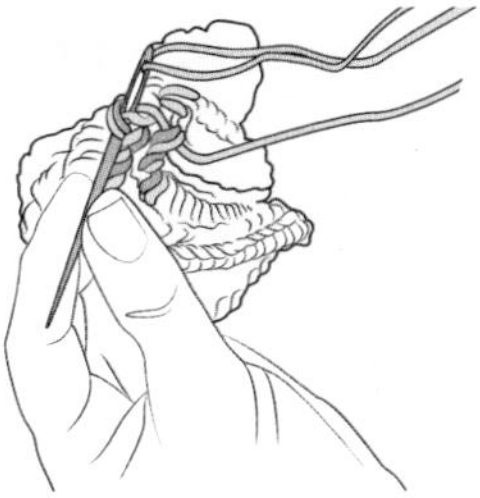

4b

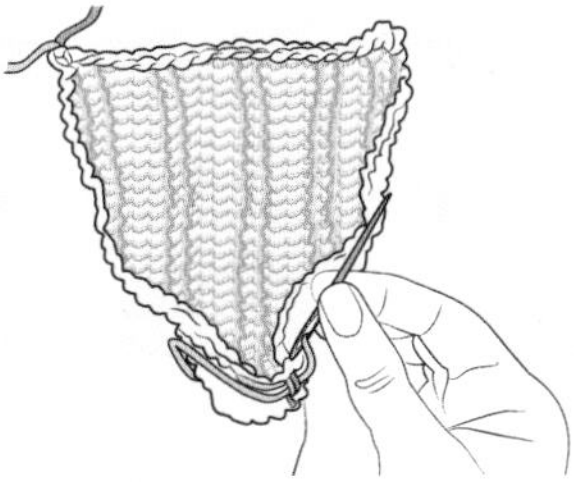

5

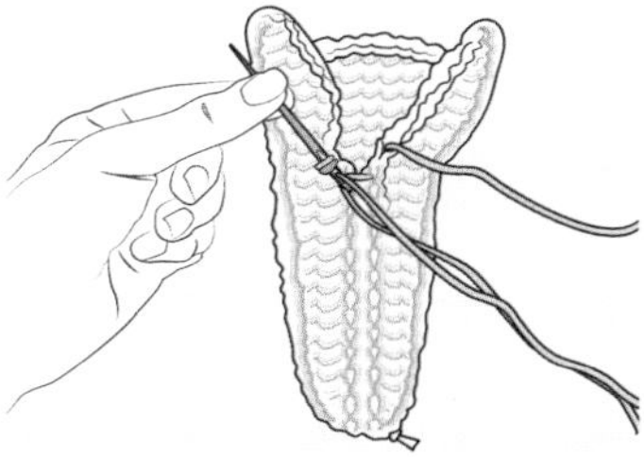

6

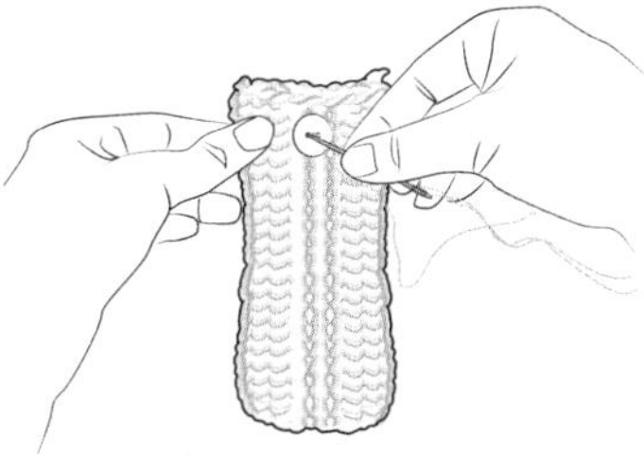

make your own yarn

Tools and materials

- Fabric Scissors
- A piece of fabric, 55 x 78cm (21¾ x 30¾in)

Upcycling has become a big part of our story and we'd like to introduce it to you, too. By using what you already have – like an unused t-shirt or spare fabric – to make yarn, you're creating something new from something discarded; thereby doing your bit to live sustainably and showcasing a meaning in everything you create.

to make

1 To begin, fold your fabric in half and trim it so that there are no frayed edges.

2 Beginning on the fold, cut 2cm (¾in) strips in the fabric, leaving 2.5cm (1in) uncut at the top/ unfolded edge of the fabric.

3 Continue to cut 2cm (¾in) wide strips across the whole fabric length; try to cut in straight and precise lines.

4 Starting on the left-hand side, working on just the top layer of the fabric, cut through the 2.5cm (1in) uncut part of the strip for every other cut made. Do this across the whole top layer.

5 On the bottom layer, you need to repeat the process described in Step 4 but cut the strips in pairs.

6 When you are finished, pick an end and start rolling the strips into a ball.

there is meaning in everything I create

1

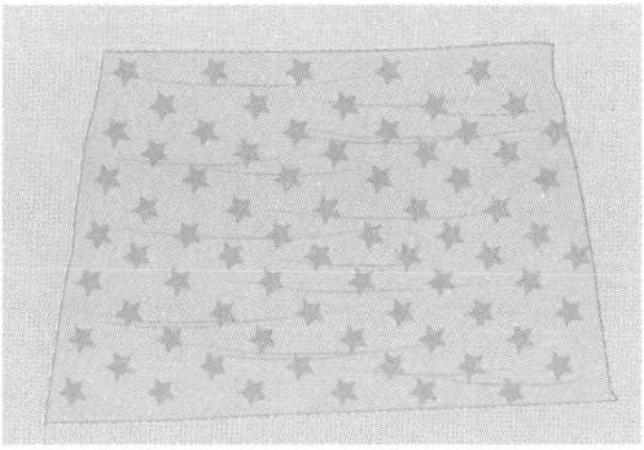

2

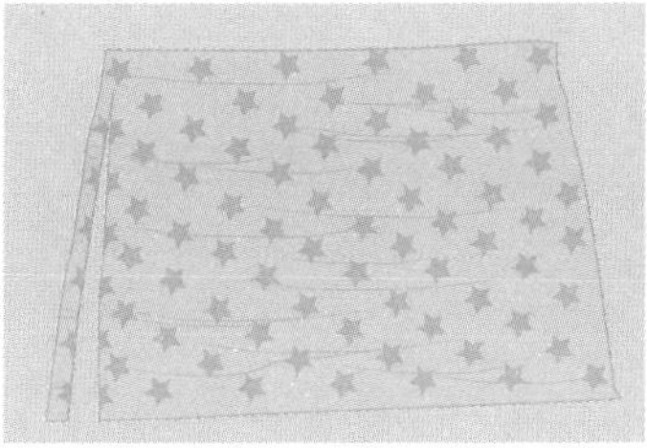

3

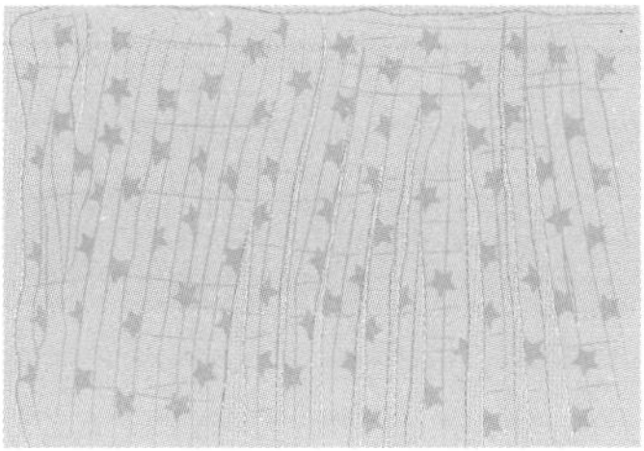

4

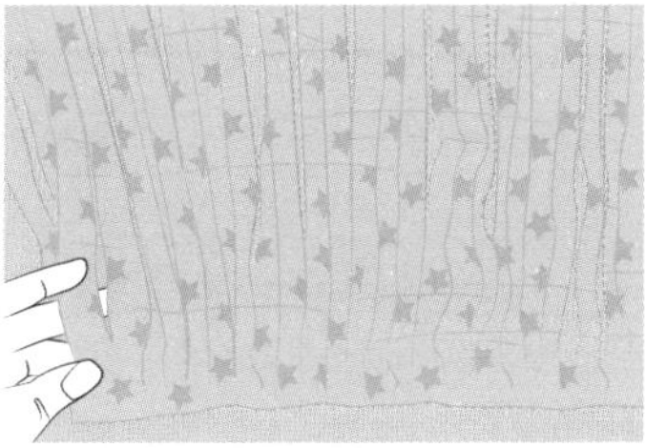

5

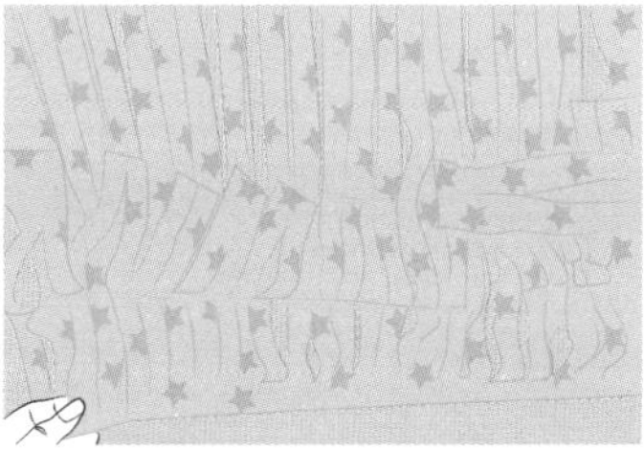

6

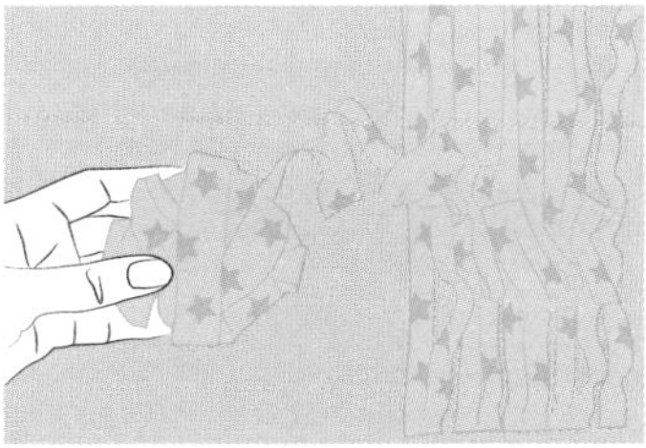

acknowledgements

Vanessa

To my husband for being the pillar of unwavering strength and love. My mother, Florence who is the strongest person in the world and my brothers Nana, Daniel and Christopher, to Hezekiah, Thyra and Zara our rays of sunshine. And my co-founder Sicgmone for inspiring me daily and being a source of constant support and inspiration. Thank you to all.

A special thanks to the Leaping Hare team: Monica Perdoni who has been our cheerleader and the publishing team, especially Charlotte Frost, who has simply transformed our writing experience for this project.

Sicgmone

I would like to say a big thank you to knitwear designers Sheree Robinson and Peju Obasa for their support with the knit projects in this book. Also, the support of all our Black Girl Knit Club members over the past few years, who have helped us to create this beautiful sisterhood of creative women. Lastly my sister Madeleine, Dad – Alex, Mum – Theresa and Brother – Daniel for always believing in my creativity and vision. You have all contributed to making this book possible.
https://www.blackgirlknitclub.com

The publisher would like to thank Rowan (www.knitrowan.com) and Cascade Yarns® (www.cascadeyarns.com) for supplying the yarn for the projects.

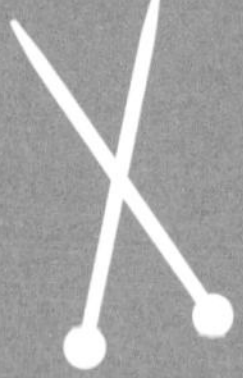